HOUGHTON MIFFLIN
Math
MATHEMATICS

Skill Workbook

Grade 1

Houghton Mifflin Company • BOSTON

Atlanta • Dallas • Geneva, Illinois • Palo Alto • Princeton

This Skill Workbook contains

- all of the Skill Worksheets from *Houghton Mifflin Mathematics Math Masters* in an easy-to-manage workbook format

- new Skill Plus Worksheets for extra practice

Illustration

Christine Czernota: pp. 30, 39, 42, 45, 51, 55, 57, 58, 60, 71, 73, 76, 78, 83, 84, 85, 89, 97, 100, 104, 108, 109, 113, 129, 130, 131, 137, 146, 147, 154, 169

Copyright © 1995 by Houghton Mifflin Company.
All Rights Reserved.

No part of this work may be reproduced or transmitted in any form or by any means, electronic or mechanical, including photocopying and recording, or by any information storage or retrieval system without the prior written permission of Houghton Mifflin Company unless such copying is expressly permitted by federal copyright law. Address inquiries to School Permissions, Houghton Mifflin Company, 222 Berkeley Street, Boston, MA 02116-3764.

Printed in U.S.A.

ISBN: 0-395-68007-7

456789-BBS-98 97 96

Skill Workbook

Table of Contents

	Page
Skill Worksheets (1 through 26)	1
Skill Plus Worksheets (1 through 144)	27

Worksheet-to-Lesson Correlation

Module 1

Lesson	Skill Plus Worksheet
1*	1
2	2, 3
3	4
4	5
5	6
6	7
7	8
8	9, 10
9	11
10	12
11	13
12	14
13	15
14	16
15	17, 18

Module 2

Lesson	Skill Plus Worksheet
1	19
2	20
3	21
4	22
5	23, 24
6	25
7	26
8	27
9	28
10	29
11	30
12	31
13	32
14	33
15	34

Module 3

Lesson	Skill Plus Worksheet
1	35
2	36, 37
3	38
4	39
5	40
6	41
7	42
8	43, 44
9	45
10	46
11	47
12	48
13	49
4	50
15	51

* Lesson 1 also contains handwriting Skill Worksheets 1 and 2. Other Skill Worksheets begin in Module 6.

Skill Workbook

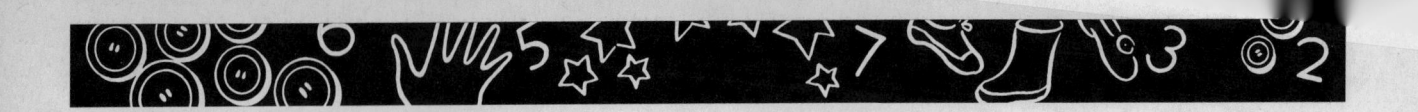

Worksheet-to-Lesson Correlation

Module 4

Lesson	Skill Plus Worksheet
1	52
2	53
3	54
4	55, 56
5	57
6	58
7	59
8	60
9	61
10	62
11	63
12	64
13	65
14	66
15	67

Module 5

Lesson	Skill Plus Worksheet
1	68
2	69
3	70
4	71, 72
5	73
6	74
7	75
8	76
9	77
10	78
11	79
12	80
13	81
14	82
15	83

Skill Workbook

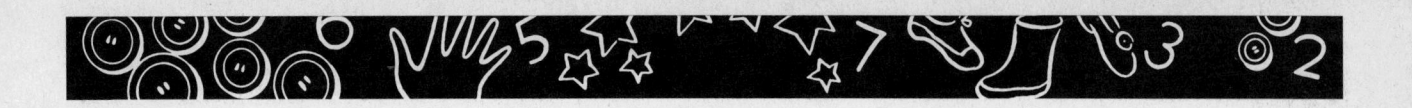

Worksheet-to-Lesson Correlation

Module 6

Lesson	Skill Worksheet	Skill Plus Worksheet
1	3	84
2		85
3		86
4	4	87
5		88
6		89
7		90, 91
8		92
9	5	93
10	6	94
11		95
12	7	96
13		97
14		98
15	8	99

Module 7

Lesson	Skill Worksheet	Skill Plus Worksheet
1		100
2	9	101
3		102
4	10	103
5		104
6		105
7	11	106
8	12	107, 108
9		109
10		110
11	13	111
12	14	112-113
13		114
14		115

Skill Workbook

Worksheet-to-Lesson Correlation

Module 8
Section A

Lesson	Skill Worksheet	Skill Plus Worksheet
1	15	116
2		117
3		118
4		119
5	16	120
6	17	121
7		122
8	18	123
9		124, 125
10	19	126
11	20	127
12		128
13		129

Module 9

Lesson	Skill Worksheet	Skill Plus Worksheet
1	21	130
2		131
3	22	132
4		133
5		134
6		135
7	23	136
8	24	137
9		138
10		139
11	25	140
12		141
13		142
14	26	143
15		144

Name _____

SKILL WORKSHEET 1

Write the number.

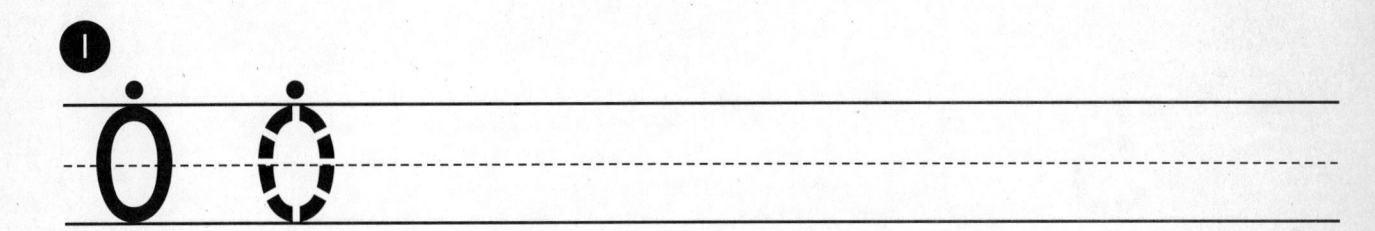

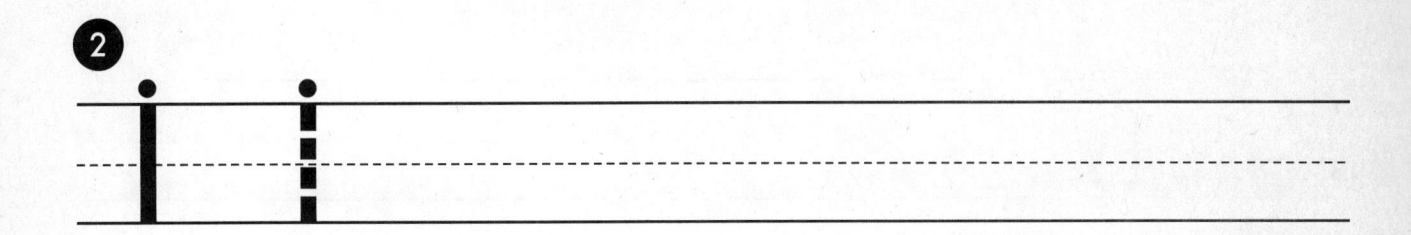

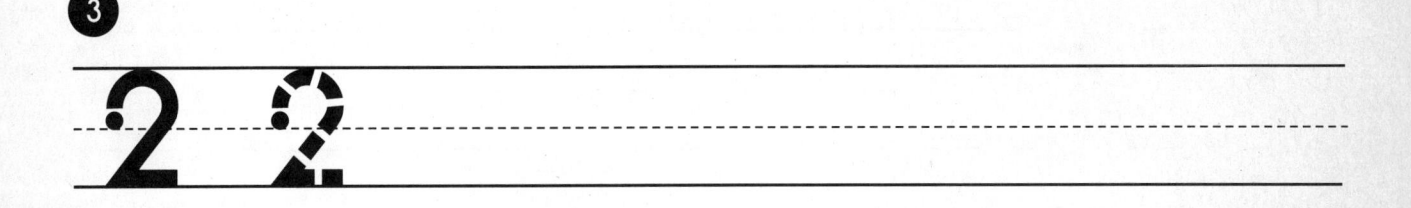

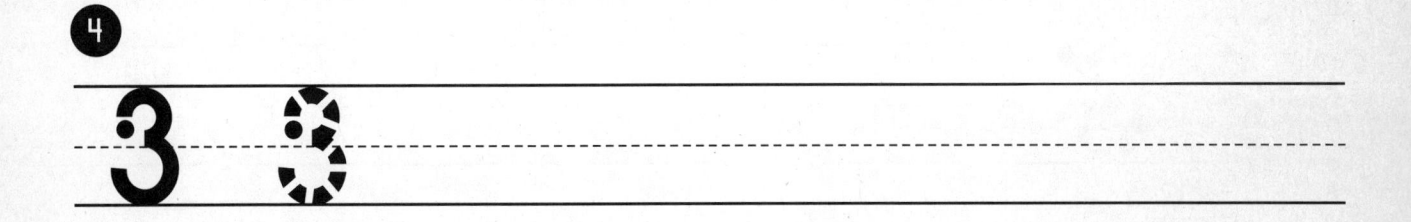

❶ 0 0

❷ 1 1

❸ 2 2

❹ 3 3

❺ 4 4

© Houghton Mifflin Company. All rights reserved/1

Module 1: Section A, Lesson 1

Name _____

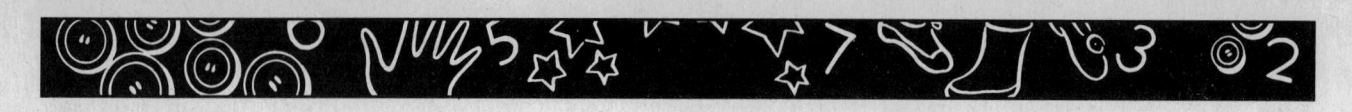

SKILL WORKSHEET 2

Write the number.

1. 5 5

2. 6 6

3. 7 7

4. 8 8

5. 9 9

2 Module 1: Section A, Lesson 1   © Houghton Mifflin Company. All rights reserved/1

Name _____

Materials: Counters

1 Draw a picture for each double.

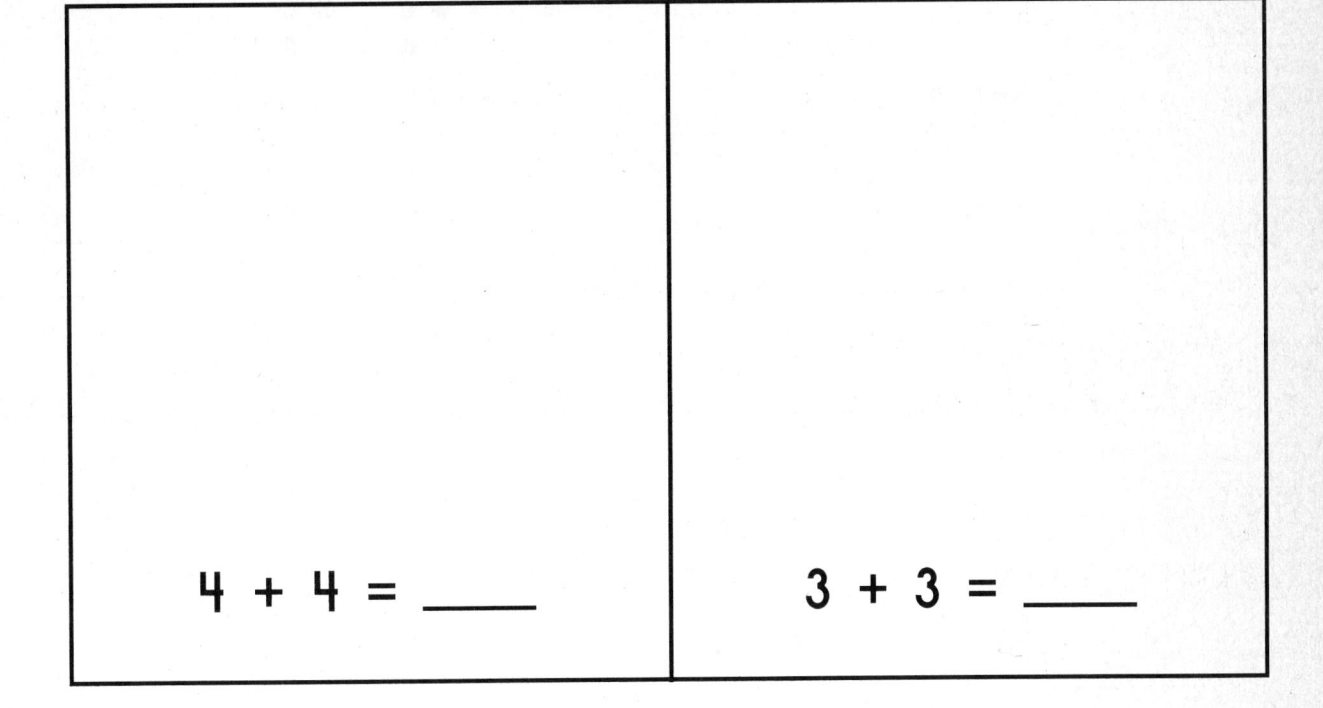

4 + 4 = ___   3 + 3 = ___

Use counters.
Show the doubles.
Add.

2 1 + 1 = _2_   5 + 5 = ___   3 + 3 = ___

3 6 + 6 = ___   7 + 7 = ___   9 + 9 = ___

4 2 + 2 = ___   4 + 4 = ___   8 + 8 = ___

Name _____

SKILL 4 WORKSHEET

Write all the fact family sentences.

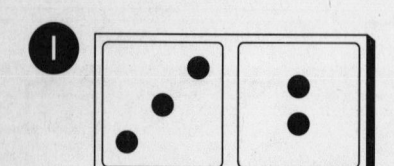

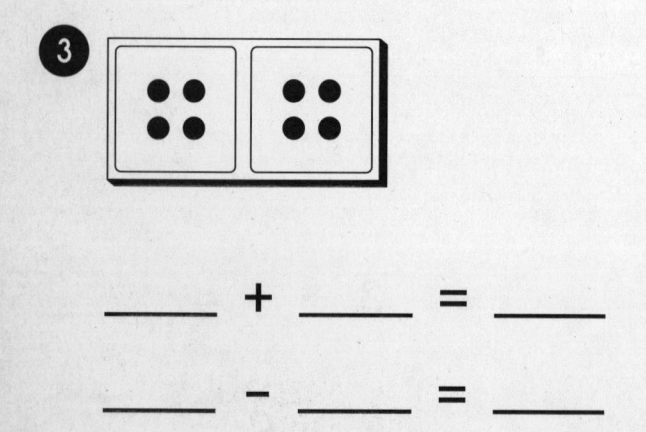

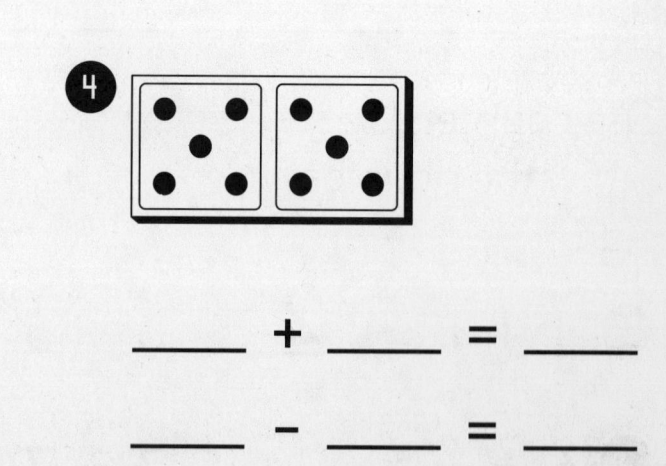

1. [domino: 4 dots | 2 dots]

___ + ___ = ___

___ + ___ = ___

___ - ___ = ___

___ - ___ = ___

2. [domino: 6 dots | 4 dots]

___ + ___ = ___

___ + ___ = ___

___ - ___ = ___

___ - ___ = ___

3. [domino: 5 dots | 5 dots]

___ + ___ = ___

___ - ___ = ___

4. [domino: 5 dots | 5 dots]

___ + ___ = ___

___ - ___ = ___

4 Module 6: Section A, Lesson 4 © Houghton Mifflin Company. All rights reserved/1

Name _____

Draw more pennies to make 10¢.
Write the missing number.

1.

6¢ + __4__ ¢ = 10¢

2.

8¢ + _____ ¢ = 10¢

3.

5¢ + _____ ¢ = 10¢

4.

7¢ + _____ ¢ = 10¢

Name _____

SKILL WORKSHEET 6

Materials: play money or punch-out pennies and dimes

Use coins.
Find out how much change.

Each child has a 🪙.

1. Mary buys ▱ 7¢.

Her change is _____ ¢.

2. Mike buys ✏️ 4¢.

His change is _____ ¢.

3. Lani buys 🖍 6¢.

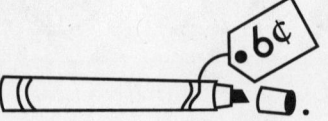

Her change is _____ ¢.

4. Jake buys 📎 9¢.

His change is _____ ¢.

6   Module 6: Section B, Lesson 10   © Houghton Mifflin Company. All rights reserved/1

Name _____

SKILL 7 WORKSHEET

1 Ring a group of ten houses.
Estimate how many houses there are in all.

About _____ houses.

2 Tally the houses.

3 How many houses are there in all?
_____

© Houghton Mifflin Company. All rights reserved/1   Module 6: Section C, Lesson 12   7

Name _____

Use the grid.
Find the missing numbers.

+	0	1	2	3	4	5
0	0	1	2	3	4	5
1	1	2	3	4	5	6
2	2	3	4	5	6	7
3	3	4	5	6	7	8
4	4	5	6	7	8	9
5	5	6	7	8	9	10

①
  4   5
+ ___   + 4   + ___   + 3
 ___   ___   ___   ___
  8   7   10   8

②
___ + 0 = 0   3 + 3 = ___   ___ + 1 = 2

③
___ + 5 = 10   3 + 1 = ___   2 + ___ = 7

④ Ring all the problems that are doubles.

8 Module 6: Section C, Lesson 15   © Houghton Mifflin Company. All rights reserved/1

Name _____

Ring the tens to help you count.

①

Tens	Ones

In All

②

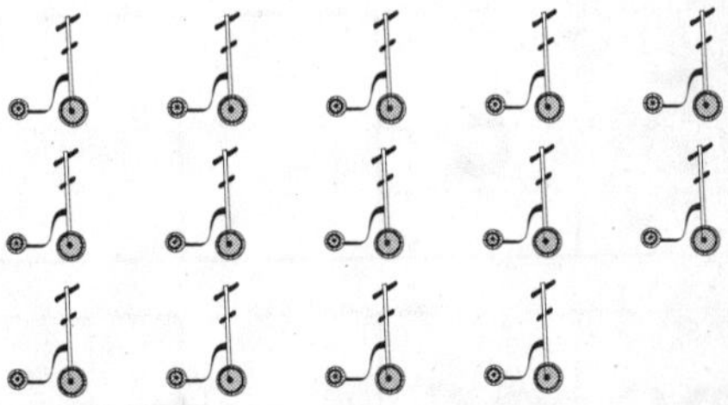

Tens	Ones

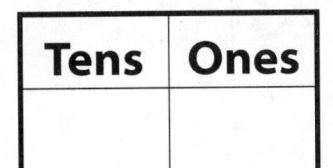

In All

③

Tens	Ones

In All

④

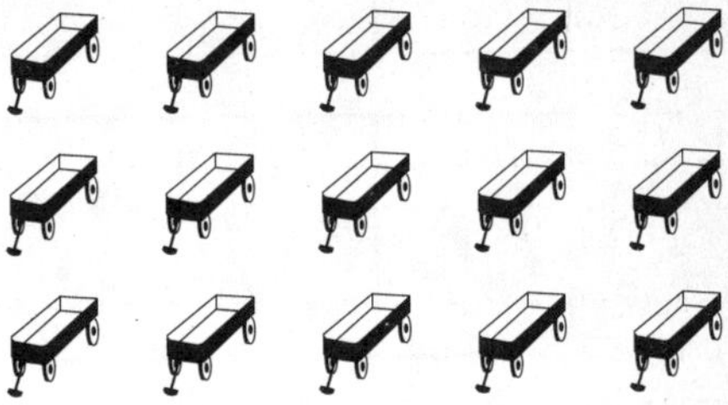

Tens	Ones

In All

⑤

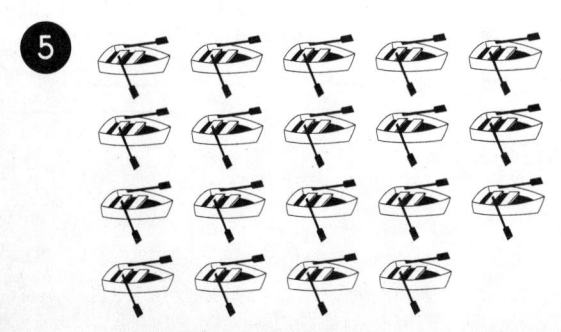

Tens	Ones

In All

⑥

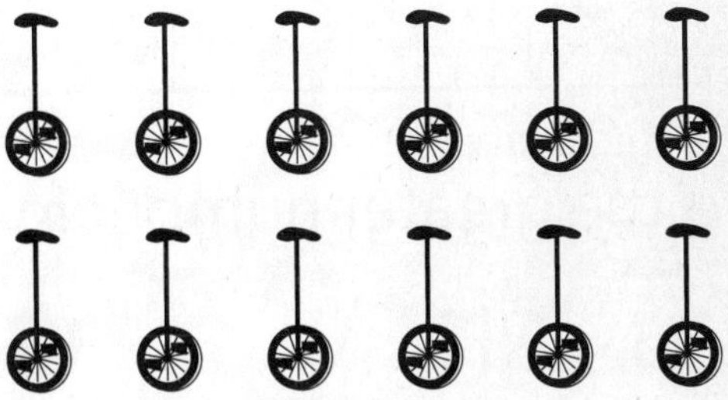

Tens	Ones

In All

© Houghton Mifflin Company. All rights reserved/1

Name _____

Fill in the missing numbers.

1) | 5 | 6 | 7 | | | 10 | | | 13 | |

2) | 22 | 23 | | | | 27 | | | 30 | |

3) | 41 | | | 44 | | | 47 | 48 | | 50 |

4) | 85 | 86 | | 88 | | 90 | 91 | 92 | | |

5) | 67 | 68 | 69 | | 71 | | 73 | | | |

6) | 13 | | | 16 | | | 19 | | 21 | |

Ring the greater number in each group.

7) 23 24   8) 65 85

9) 18 35   10) 42 57

10   Module 7: Section A, Lesson 4   © Houghton Mifflin Company. All rights reserved/1

Name _____

Find the value of each group of coins.

1. _____ ¢

2. _____ ¢

3. _____ ¢

4. _____ ¢

5. _____ ¢

© Houghton Mifflin Company. All rights reserved/1

Module 7: Section B, Lesson 7

Name _____

**Which coins will you use to pay for the seeds?
Match by drawing a line.**

1. SEEDS 26¢

   a.  [dime, dime, dime, nickel, nickel, nickel, penny, penny]

2. SEEDS 20¢

   b.  [dime, penny, penny, penny]

3. SEEDS 47¢

   c.  [dime, dime, penny, penny, penny, penny, penny, penny]

4. SEEDS 13¢

   d.  [dime, nickel, nickel]

12   Module 7: Section B, Lesson 8   © Houghton Mifflin Company. All rights reserved/1

Name _____

Materials: Centimeter ruler

Measure with a centimeter ruler.

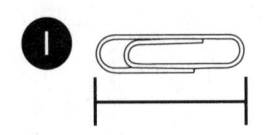

1. _____ centimeters

2. 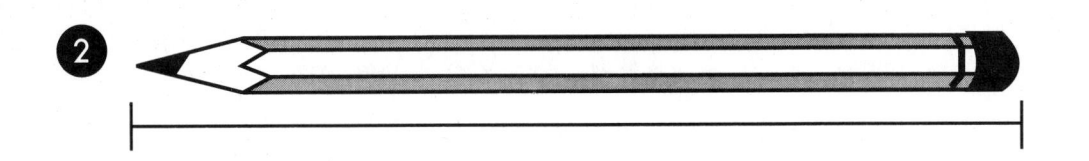 _____ centimeters

3. 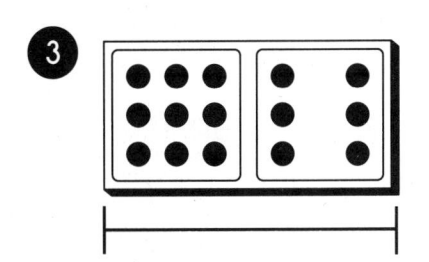 _____ centimeters

4. 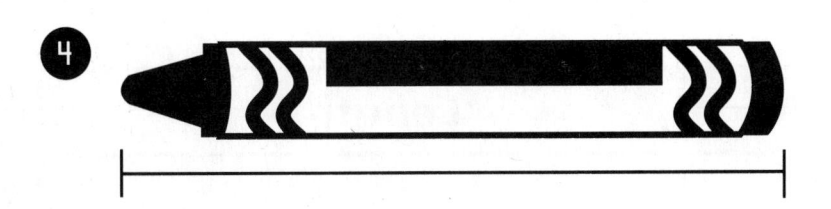 _____ centimeters

5.  _____ centimeters

Module 7: Section C, Lesson 11

Name _____

Skill 14 Worksheet

Materials: Centimeter ruler

Find these objects in the classroom.
Measure the length with a centimeter ruler.

1 crayon

_____ centimeters

2 pencil

_____ centimeters

3 shoe

_____ centimeters

4 scissors

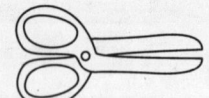

_____ centimeters

5 marker

_____ centimeters

6 paintbrush

_____ centimeters

7 Choose another object.
Measure the length. Draw it.

What I Measured	Length
	_____ centimeters

14   Module 7: Section C, Lesson 12   © Houghton Mifflin Company. All rights reserved/1

Name _____

Name the shapes.

1 I am a _____.

　　I have _____ sides.

　　I have _____ corners.

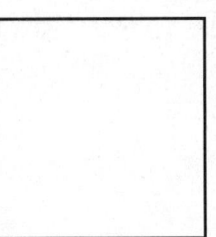

2 I am a _____.

　　I have _____ sides.

　　I have _____ corners.

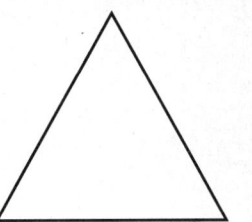

3 I am a _____.

　　I have _____ sides.

　　I have _____ corners.

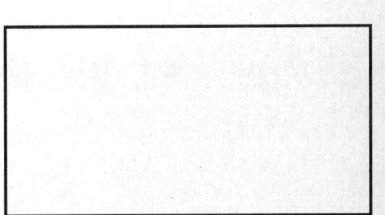

Name _____

SKILL 16 WORKSHEET

Ring the items.

1 Show **2** equal parts.

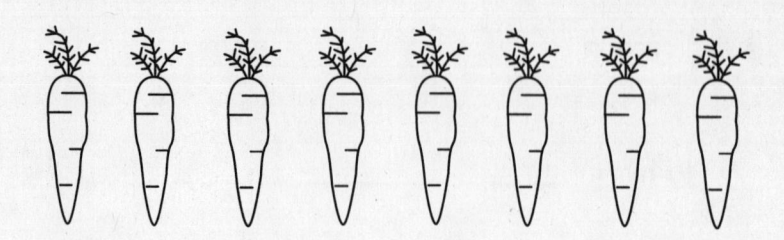

2 Show **3** equal parts.

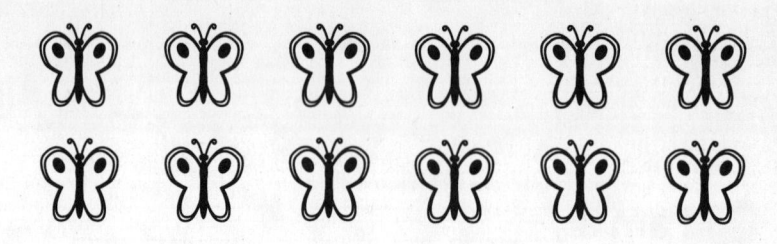

3 Show **4** equal parts.

4 Show **2** equal parts.

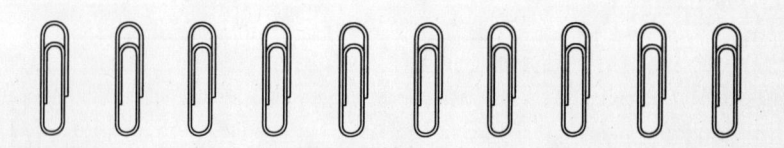

5 Show **2** equal parts.

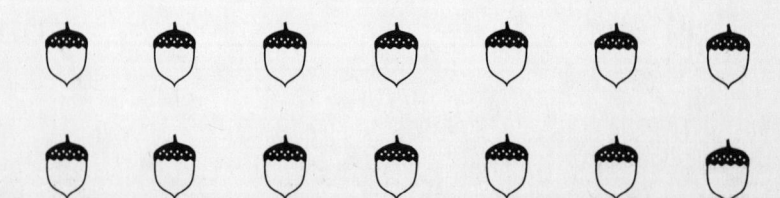

16 Module 8: Section A, Lesson 5   © Houghton Mifflin Company. All rights reserved/1

Name _____

Read the thermometer.
Write the temperature.

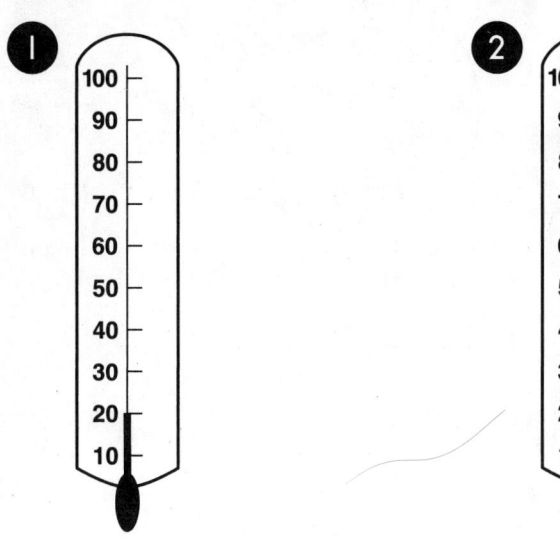

1 ____ degrees

2 ____ degrees

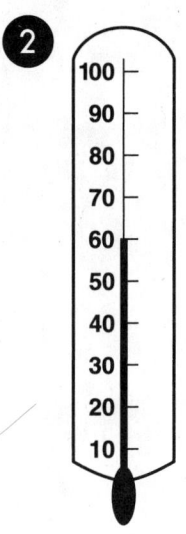

3 ____ degrees

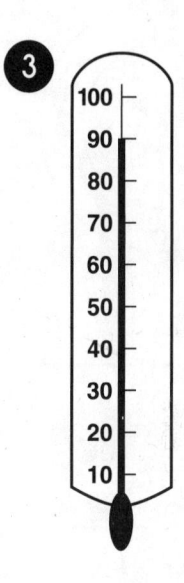

4 ____ degrees

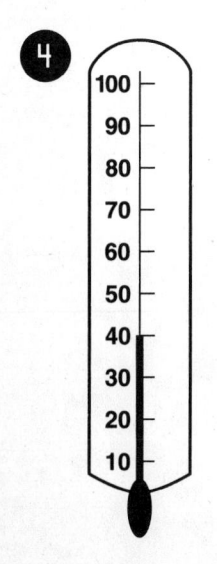

5 ____ degrees

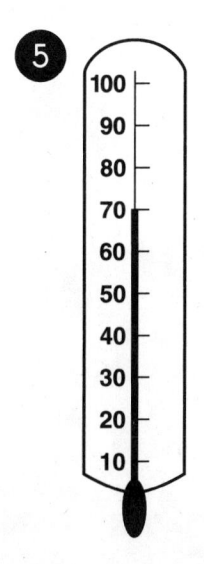

6 ____ degrees

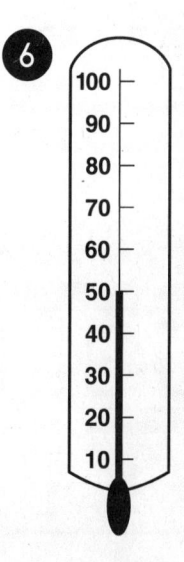

Name ____________________

SKILL 18 WORKSHEET

Write the time.

1

___ : ___

2

___ : ___

3

___ : ___

4

___ : ___

5

___ : ___

6

___ : ___

© Houghton Mifflin Company. All rights reserved/1

Name _____

Measure with an inch ruler.
Write the length.

1

_____ inches

2

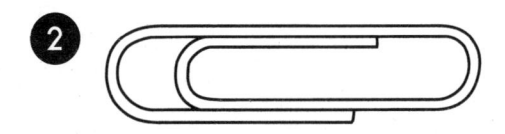

_____ inches

3

_____ inches

4

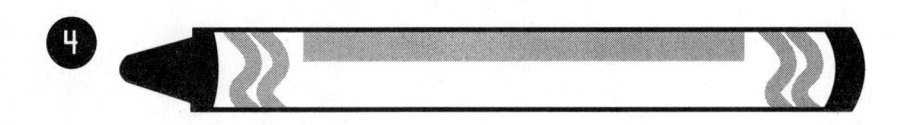

_____ inches

Name _____

Ring the one that is heavier.

1. pebble   brick

2. cup of feathers   cup of sand

3. hammer   nail

4. bicycle   car

Ring the one that is lighter.

5. apple   watermelon

6. toy balloon   basketball

7. telephone pole   fishing pole

8. bucket of water   bucket of popcorn

Name _____

Skill Worksheet 21

Count on 1, 2, or 3.
Find the sum.

1.
5 + 2 = 7
7 + 3
1 + 9
3 + 2
2 + 8
7 + 1

2.
4 + 3
2 + 6
1 + 5
3 + 8
4 + 1
3 + 3

3.
6 + 1
8 + 2
5 + 3
4 + 2
3 + 6
2 + 2

4.
1 + 4
7 + 2
8 + 1
2 + 5
3 + 7
9 + 1

5.
1 + 2
2 + 3
3 + 4
6 + 2
1 + 8
5 + 1

© Houghton Mifflin Company. All rights reserved/1

Module 9: Section A, Lesson 1

Name _____

**Make a ten.
Find the sum.**

①   5   9   3   9   8   2
    + 8   + 2   + 8   + 4   + 5   + 9
    ——   ——   ——   ——   ——   ——
    13

②   8   3   6   9   9   8
    + 7   + 9   + 8   + 5   + 6   + 3
    ——   ——   ——   ——   ——   ——

③   9   8   9   8   8   9
    + 9   + 4   + 7   + 8   + 9   + 8
    ——   ——   ——   ——   ——   ——

④   6   9   4   7   8   7
    + 9   + 1   + 9   + 8   + 2   + 9
    ——   ——   ——   ——   ——   ——

⑤   4   5   8   9   2   5
    + 8   + 9   + 6   + 3   + 8   + 8
    ——   ——   ——   ——   ——   ——

Name _____

Skill Worksheet 23

Find the sum.

① 10 + 10 = __20__   23 + 20 = ____

② 51 + 40 = ____   12 + 10 = ____

③ 40 + 32 = ____   20 + 17 = ____

④ 55 + 30 = ____   68 + 10 = ____

⑤   10   53   65   40
  + 22   + 30   + 20   + 28
    32

⑥   50   10   42   39
  + 38   + 87   + 50   + 10

⑦   36   49   30   50
  + 20   + 10   + 24   + 17

Name _____

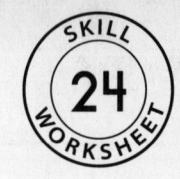

Materials: Base-ten materials

Fill in the boxes in the charts.

1 Add **7** to the numbers.

10	18	41	72	52	36
17	25				

2 Subtract **5** from the numbers.

10	15	20	25	30	35
9					

3 Add **8** to the numbers.

11	24	71	62	50	36
19					

4 Subtract **3** from the numbers.

12	28	31	40	23	27
9					

24 Module 9: Section B, Lesson 8

Name _____

Continue the pattern one more time.

1 2,   2 + 2,   2 + 2 + 2,   2 + 2 + 2 + 2,

_2 + 2 + 2 + 2 + 2_   2, 4, 6, 8, 10

2 3,   3 + 3,   3 + 3 + 3,   3 + 3 + 3 + 3,

_____   3, 6, 9, 12, _____

3 4,   4 + 4,   4 + 4 + 4,   4 + 4 + 4 + 4,

_____   4, 8, 12, 16, _____

4 5,   5 + 5,   5 + 5 + 5,   5 + 5 + 5 + 5,

_____   5, 10, 15, 20, _____

5 10,   10 + 10,   10 + 10 + 10,   10 + 10 + 10 + 10,

_____   10, 20, 30, 40, _____

© Houghton Mifflin Company. All rights reserved/1   Module 9: Section C, Lesson 11

Name _____

Write three addends that name the number.
Write 4 different combinations for each number.

1. 6   7   5

1 + 4 + 1   _____   _____

_____   _____   _____

_____   _____   _____

_____   _____   _____

2. 8   9   10

_____   _____   _____

_____   _____   _____

_____   _____   _____

_____   _____   _____

Module 9: Section C, Lesson 14

Name _____

SKILL PLUS WORKSHEET 1

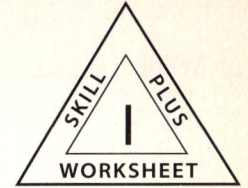

Materials: Crayons

Color.

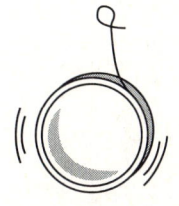

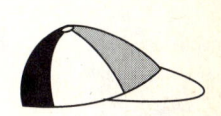

Draw a way to sort the objects.

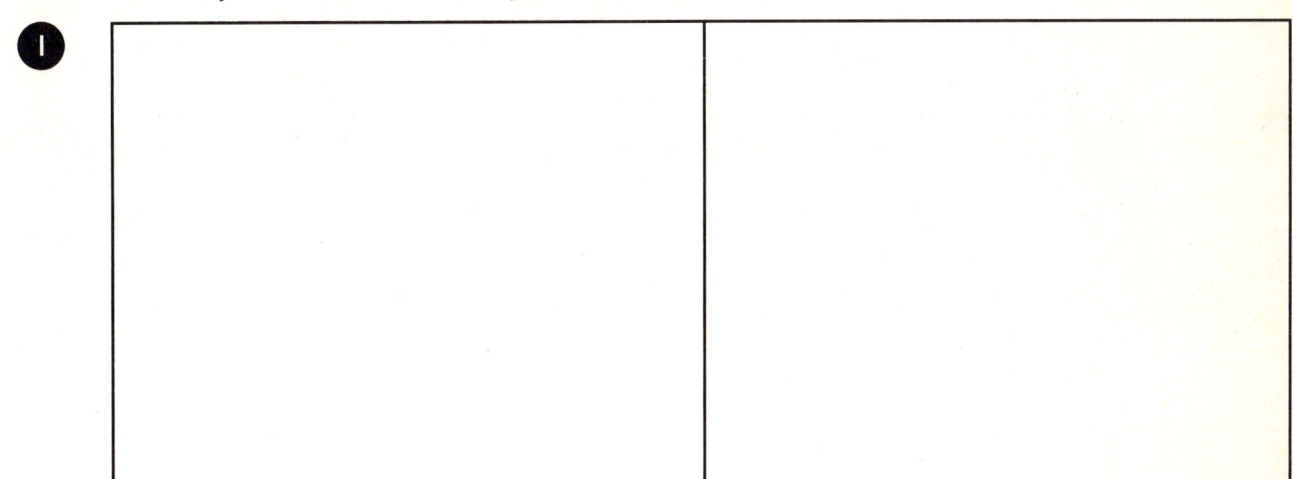

①

Draw another way to sort.

②

© Houghton Mifflin Company. All rights reserved/1

Module 1: Section A, Lesson 1   27

Name _____

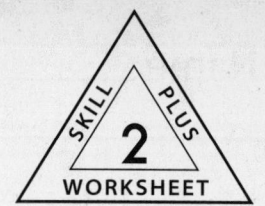

Draw each object in its group.
Then write the number of objects in the group.

Objects

Groups

1. _____ in all

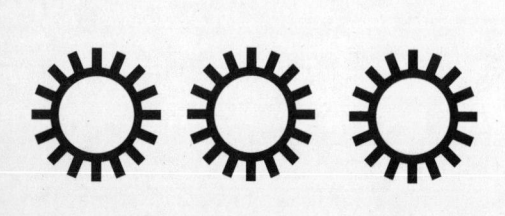

2. _____ in all

3. _____ in all

28   Module 1: Section A, Lesson 2   © Houghton Mifflin Company. All rights reserved/1

Name _____

Materials: Crayons

Draw pictures.
Write the number.

1 Draw **2** things.

2 Draw **7** things.

3 Draw **5** things.

4 Draw **9** things.

5 Draw **1** thing.

6 Draw **4** things.

7 Draw **6** things.

8 Draw **0** things.

© Houghton Mifflin Company. All rights reserved/1

Module 1: Section A, Lesson 2

Name _____

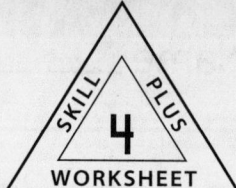

Materials: Crayons

Color the pictures.
Sort the pictures.
Draw each in its place.

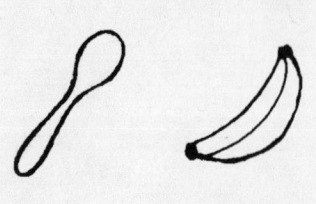

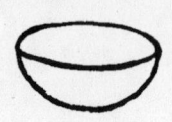

SKILL PLUS 4 WORKSHEET

Snack Time

fruits					
place setting					

Are there more fruits or place-setting items?

_____

Draw your favorite food.

30   Module 1: Section A, Lesson 3   © Houghton Mifflin Company. All rights reserved/1

Name _____

Draw the shapes in the ten-frame.
Trace the number.

1. △ △ △ △ △ △

    _6_

2. ○ ○ ○ ○ ○ ○ ○ ○ ○

    _9_

3. □ □ □ □

    _4_

© Houghton Mifflin Company. All rights reserved/1

Module 1: Section A, Lesson 4   31

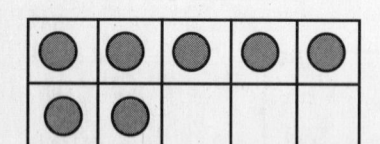

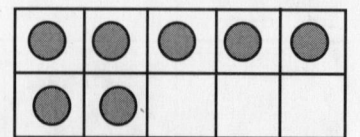

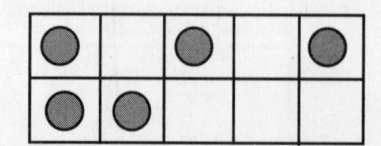

Name _____

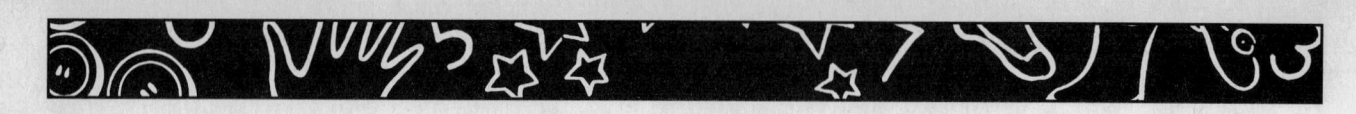

Materials: Crayons

Draw the objects in the empty ten-frame.
Make the two frames match.

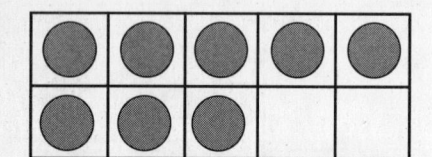

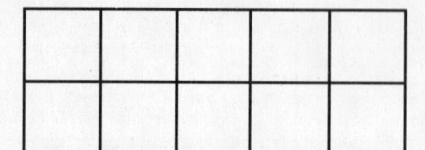

1.
2.

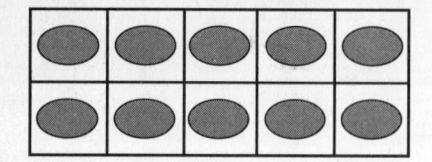

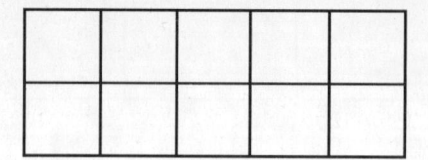

Color the frame that matches the first frame.

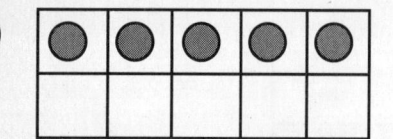

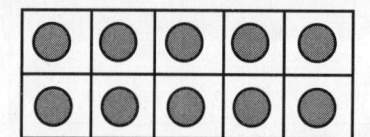

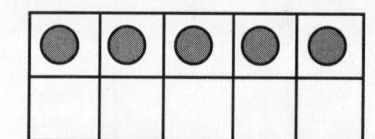

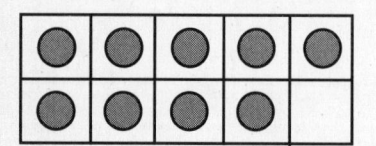

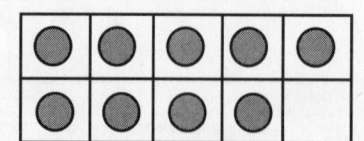

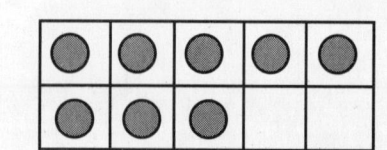

3.
4.
5.
6.

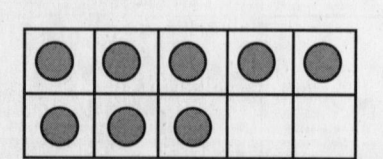

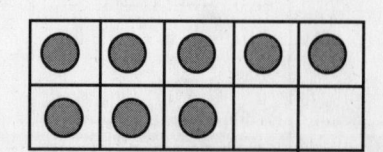

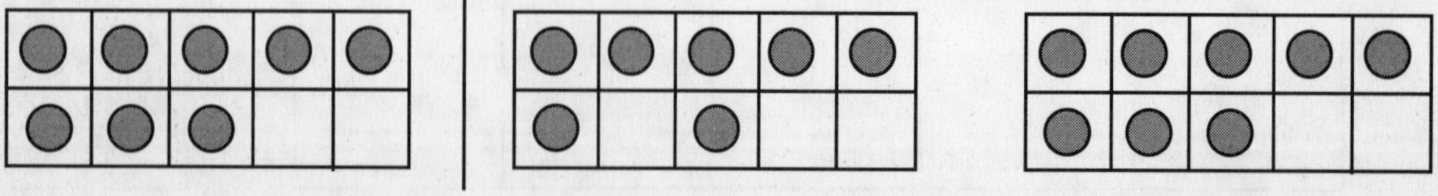

32   Module 1: Section A, Lesson 5   © Houghton Mifflin Company. All rights reserved/1

Name _____

Materials: Red, yellow, and brown crayons

Color groups of **2** red.
Color groups of **5** yellow.
Color groups of **10** brown.

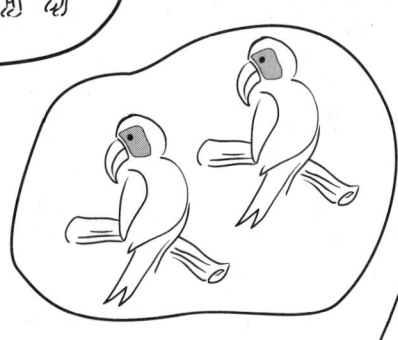

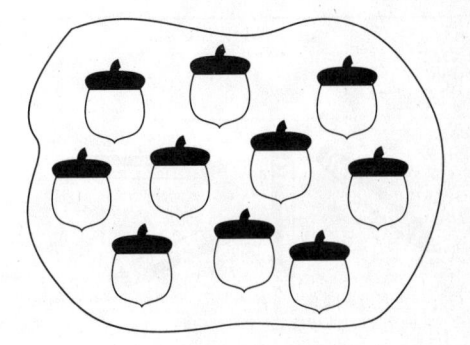

© Houghton Mifflin Company. All rights reserved/1

Module 1: Section B, Lesson 6

Name _____

Materials: Crayons

Color the objects.
Count the objects in each group.
Ring the group with more.

SKILL PLUS WORKSHEET 8

1.

2.

3.

4.

34 Module 1: Section B, Lesson 7

© Houghton Mifflin Company. All rights reserved/1

Name _____

Draw the dots in the ten-frames.
Ring the ten-frame with more.

1.

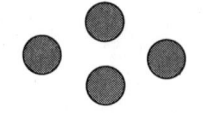

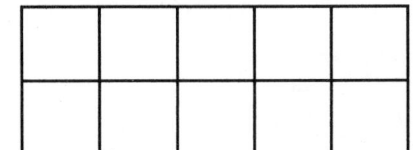

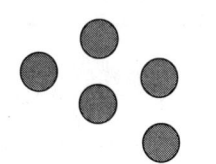

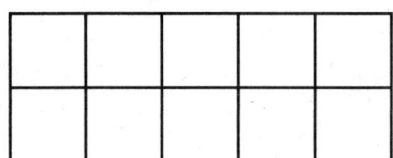

2.

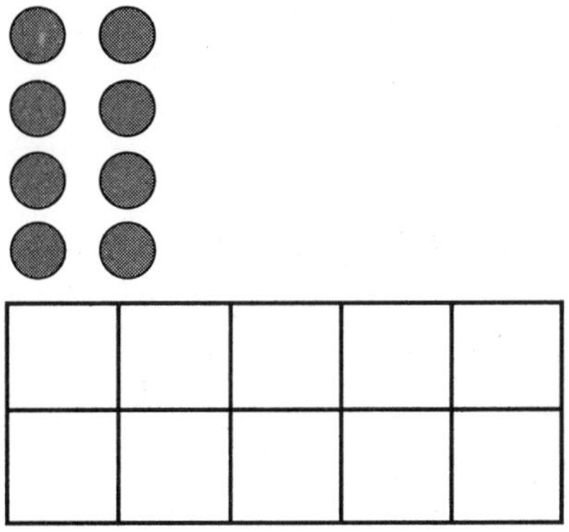

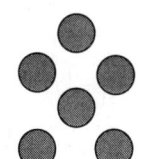

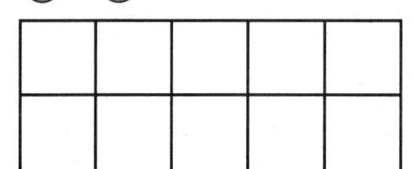

3.

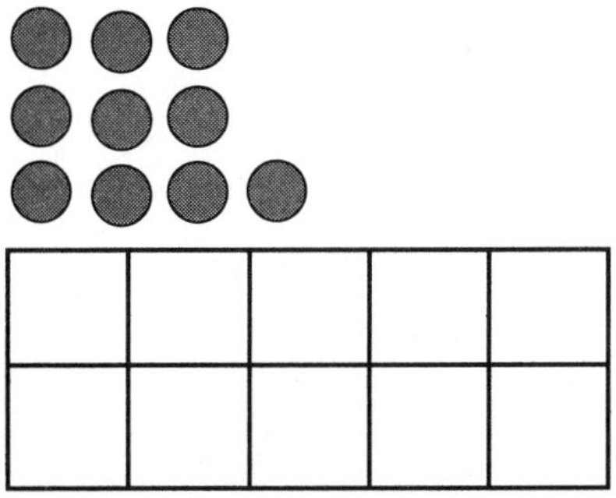

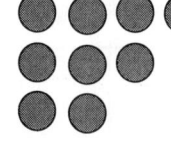

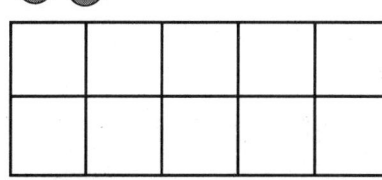

4.

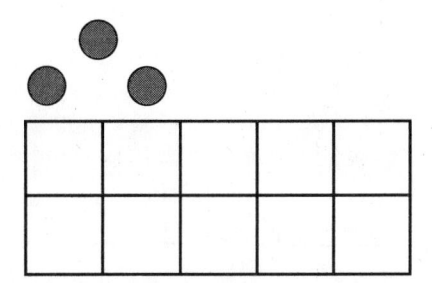

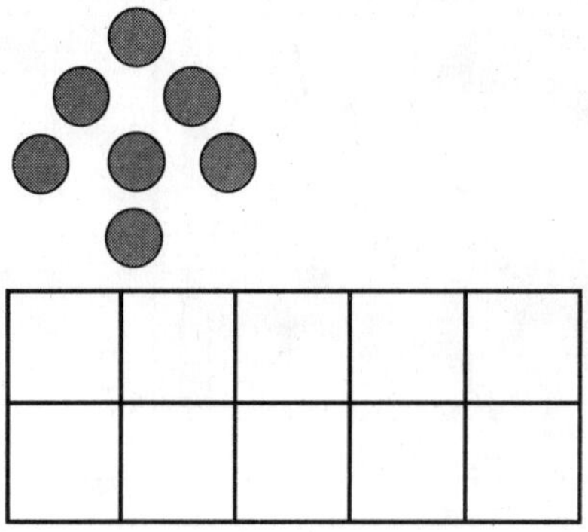

© Houghton Mifflin Company. All rights reserved/1

Module 1: Section B, Lesson 8

Name _____

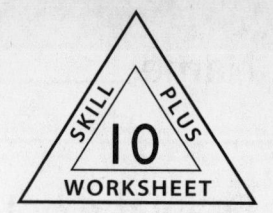

Materials: Counters of two colors

Match counters to the cubes shown.
Write the number in all.

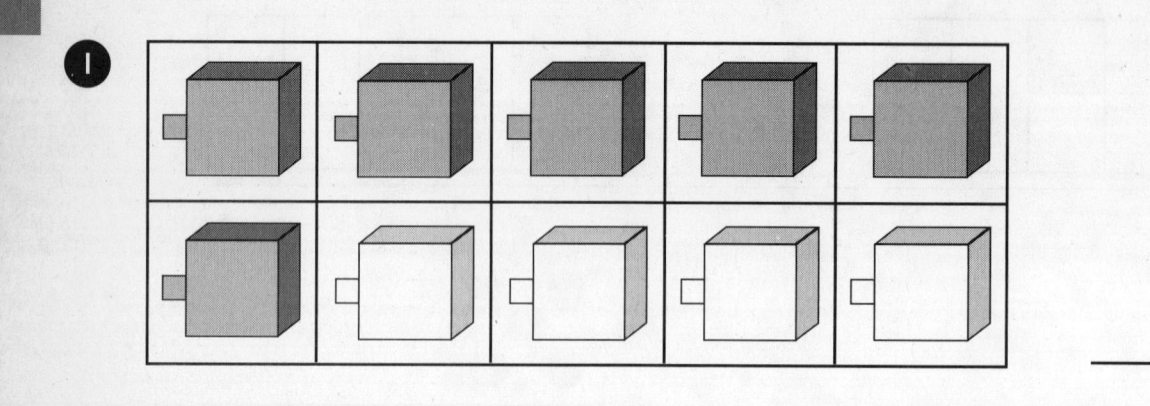

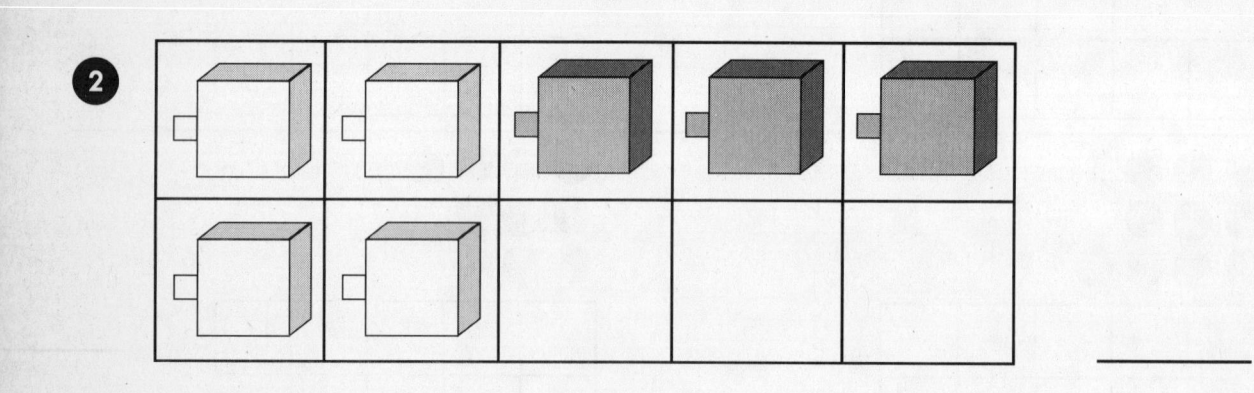

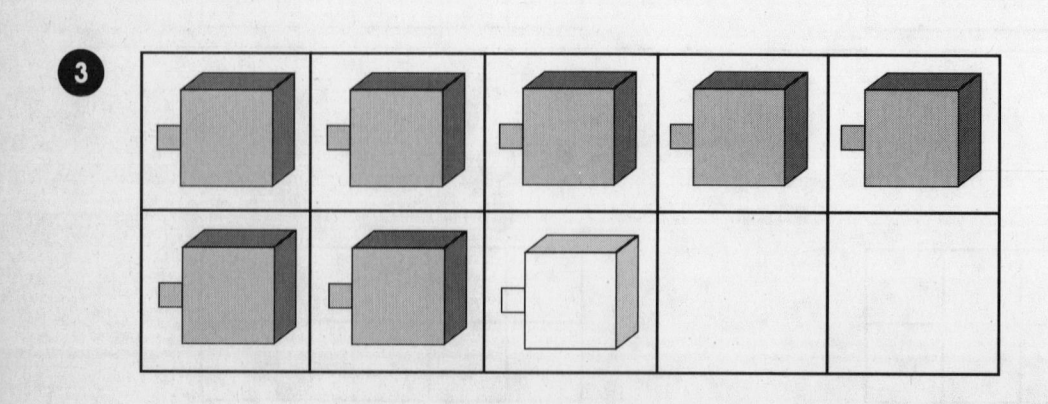

36   Module 1: Section B, Lesson 8   © Houghton Mifflin Company. All rights reserved/1

Name _____

Materials: Interlocking cubes

Make a cube train to measure the object.
Draw your cubes. Color.

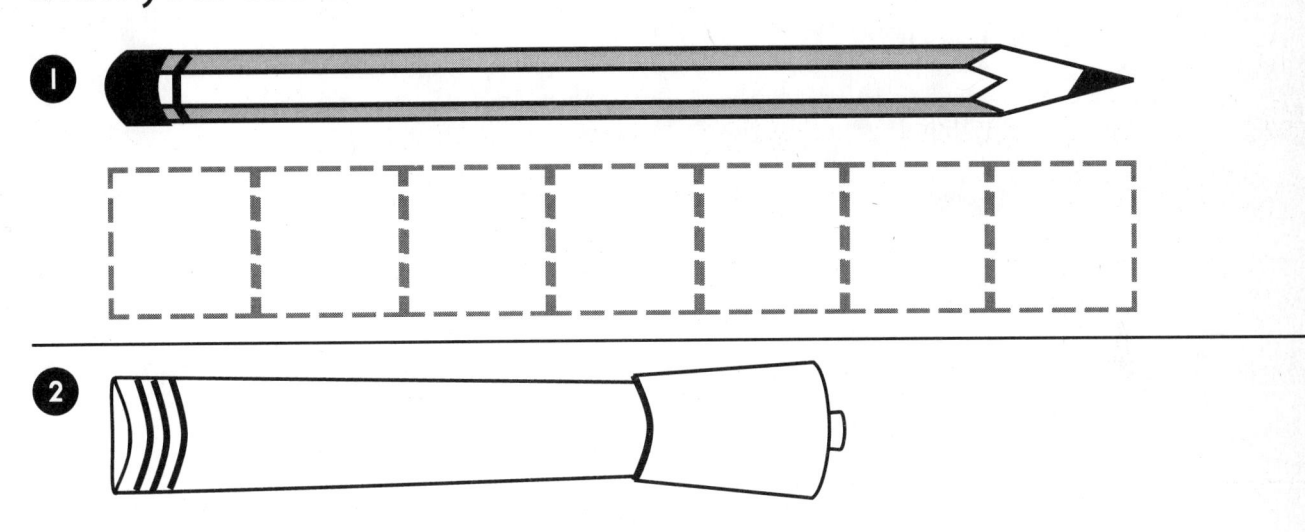

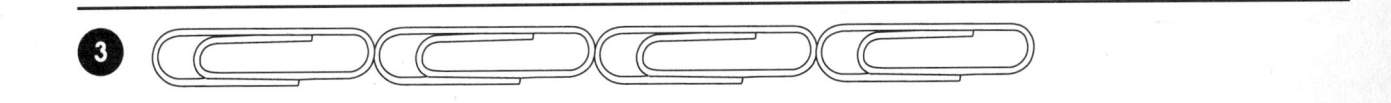

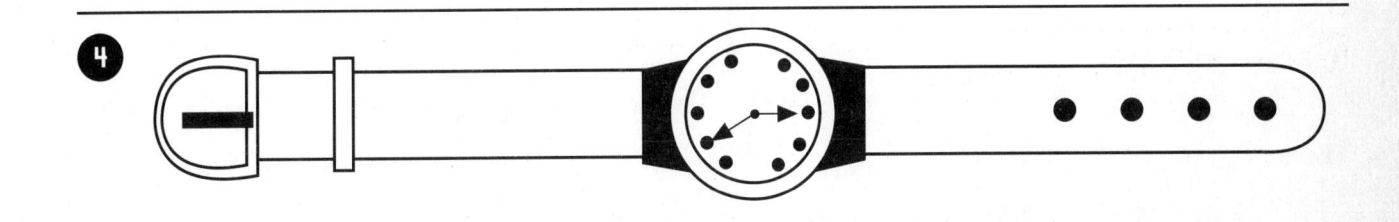

1.

2.

3.

4.

Module 1: Section B, Lesson 9

Name _____

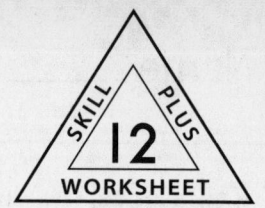

Materials: Cubes of two colors

Join the cubes in each hand.
Then join your **2** trains.
Color to show your new train.

SKILL PLUS WORKSHEET 12

1.

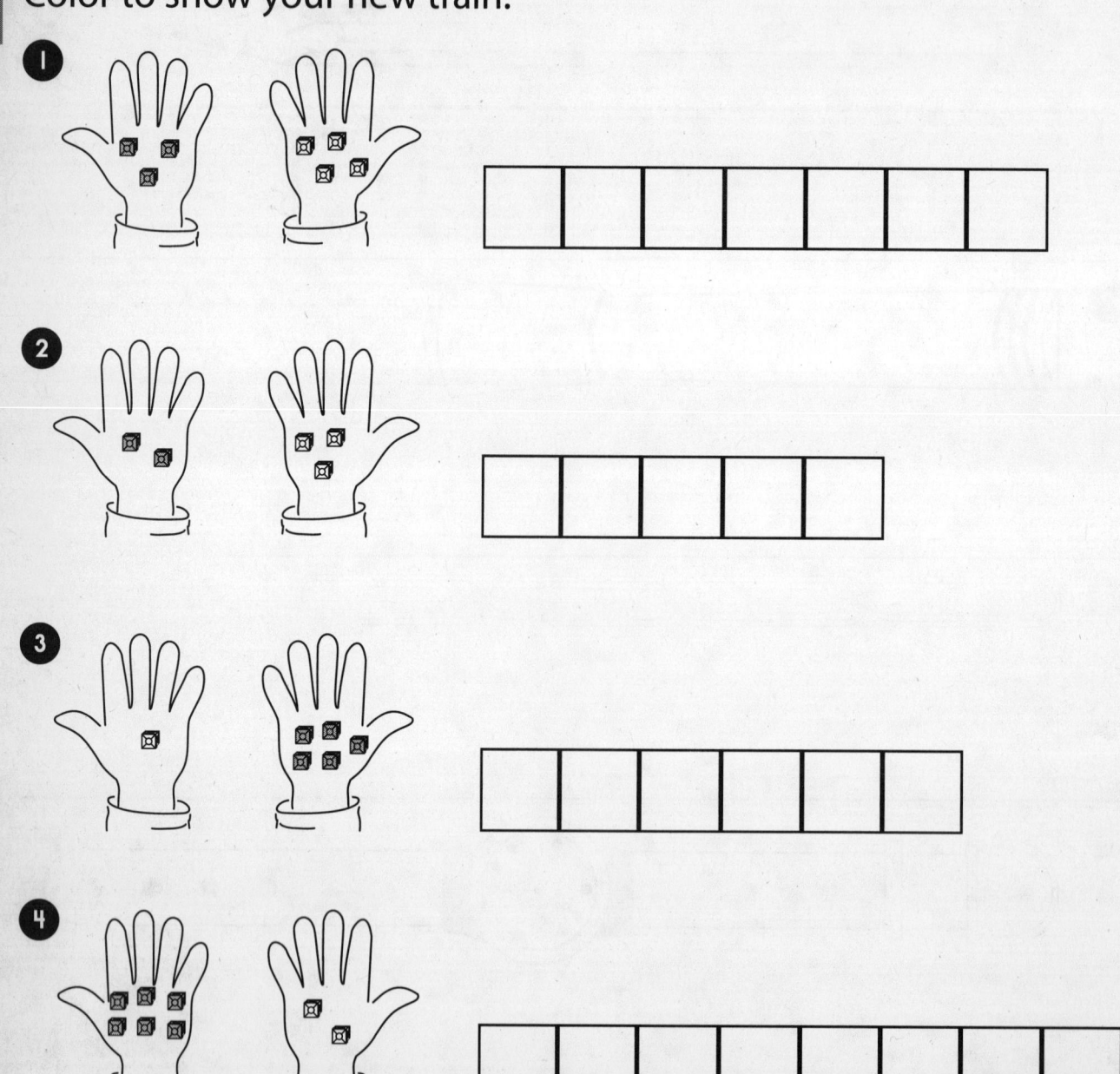

2.

3.

4.

38   Module 1: Section B, Lesson 10 © Houghton Mifflin Company. All rights reserved/1

Name _____

Materials: Crayons

Count the candles. Write the ages.
Ring the cake for the oldest person.
Color the cakes.

_____ years old    _____ years old

_____ years old

_____ years old   _____ years old

© Houghton Mifflin Company. All rights reserved/1   Module 1: Section C, Lesson 11   39

Name _____

Materials: Crayons

Color.
Read the names of the months to a partner.
Tell about the pictures.

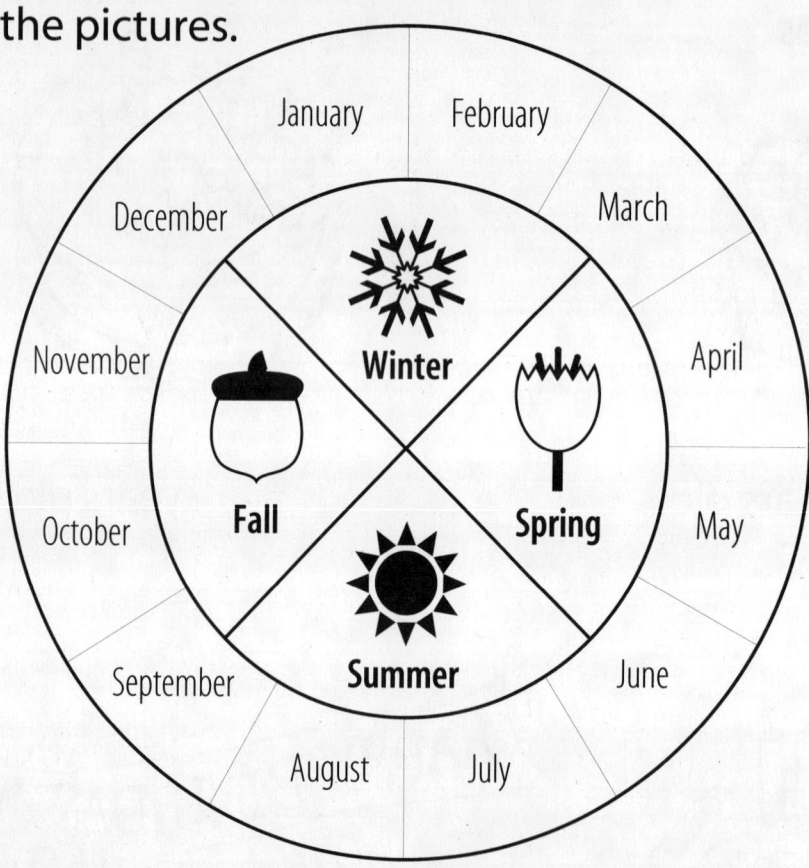

① Ring your birthday month in red.
② Ring your favorite month in brown.
③ Ring this month in blue.
④ Write about things that happen this month.

_____

_____

40   Module 1: Section C, Lesson 12   © Houghton Mifflin Company. All rights reserved/1

Name _____

Materials: Crayons

Draw pictures of things you do during the week.

| Sunday | Monday |

| Tuesday | Wednesday | Thursday |

| Friday | Saturday |

Ring your favorite day.

© Houghton Mifflin Company. All rights reserved/1

Module 1: Section C, Lesson 13 41

Name _____

Materials: Crayons

Color.
Tell a partner about each picture.

How do we use calendars?
Draw and write. _____

_____

_____

42   Module 1: Section C, Lesson 14   © Houghton Mifflin Company. All rights reserved/1

Name _____

Materials: Crayons

Draw yourself at each age.

1 as a baby

2 now

3 in high school

4 grown up

5 What can you do now that a baby can not do?

_____

_____

6 What will you do when you grow up?

_____

_____

© Houghton Mifflin Company. All rights reserved/1

Module 1: Section C, Lesson 15   43

Name _____

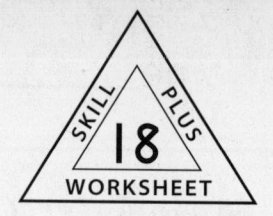

Mark any of the days to help you solve.

1 Joan did not sing on **3** of the days.
On how many days did Joan sing?

    Sunday   Monday   Tuesday
Wednesday   Thursday   Friday   Saturday   _____ days

2 Reggie drew boats on **2** of the days.
He drew airplanes on **5** of the days.
On how many days did Reggie draw?

    Sunday   Monday   Tuesday
Wednesday   Thursday   Friday   Saturday   _____ days

3 Four days were sunny.
On how many days was it cloudy?

    Sunday   Monday   Tuesday
Wednesday   Thursday   Friday   Saturday   _____ days

4 Pearl did not swim on **4** days.
On how many days did Pearl swim?

    Sunday   Monday   Tuesday
Wednesday   Thursday   Friday   Saturday   _____ days

Name _____

Materials: Crayons

Ring designs that have symmetry.
Color them red and yellow.
Color the other designs orange.

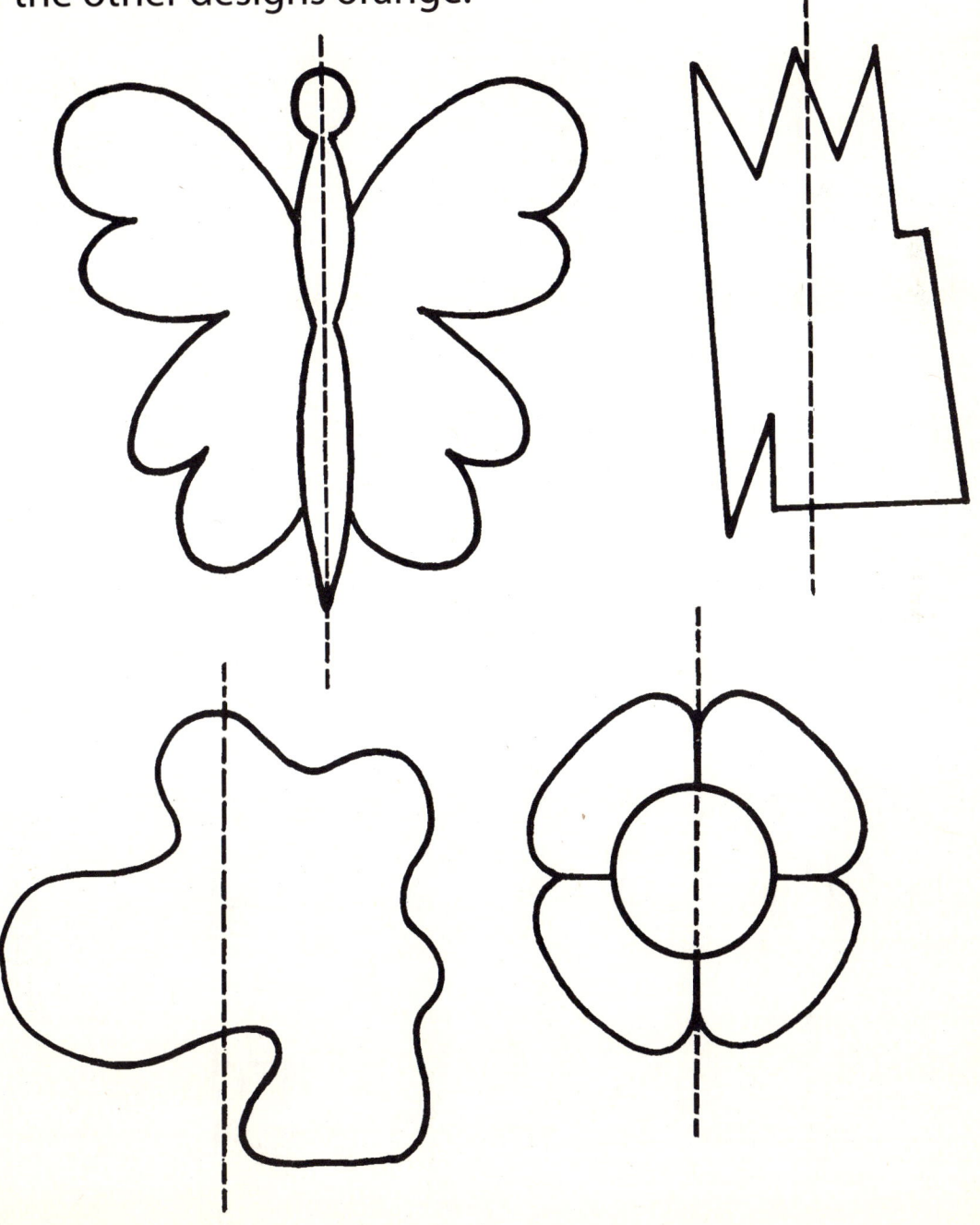

© Houghton Mifflin Company. All rights reserved/1

Module 2: Section A, Lesson 1   45

Name _____

Materials: Crayons

Finish the design.
Make it have symmetry.
Color.

1

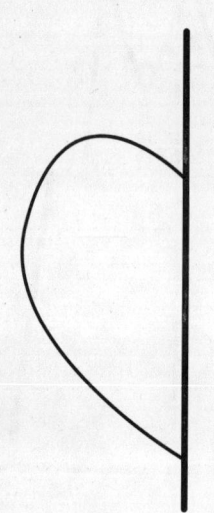

2

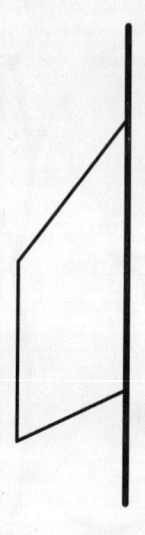

3

4

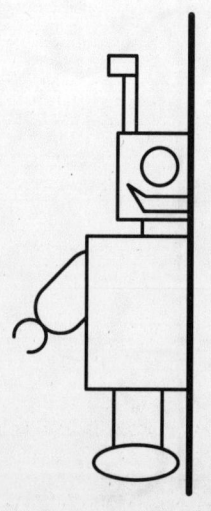

46   Module 2: Section A, Lesson 2

© Houghton Mifflin Company. All rights reserved/1

Name _____

Materials: Crayons

Draw to make designs that have symmetry.

Name _____

Materials: Crayons

Color squares.
Make designs that have symmetry.
Draw the lines of symmetry.

48 Module 2: Section A, Lesson 4 © Houghton Mifflin Company. All rights reserved/1

Name _____

**Count. Draw the double.
Write how many there are in all.**

SKILL PLUS 23 WORKSHEET

1)

_____

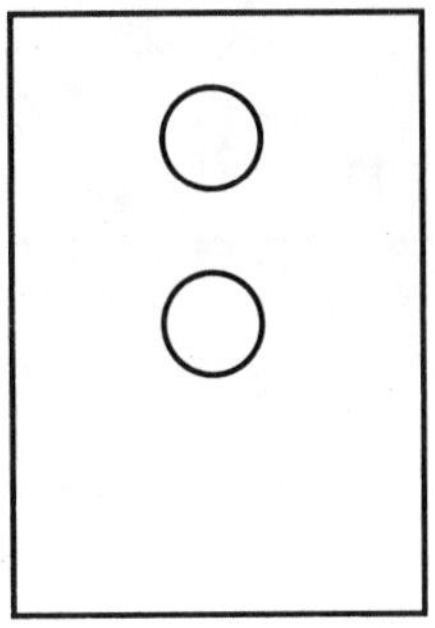

2)

_____

3)

_____

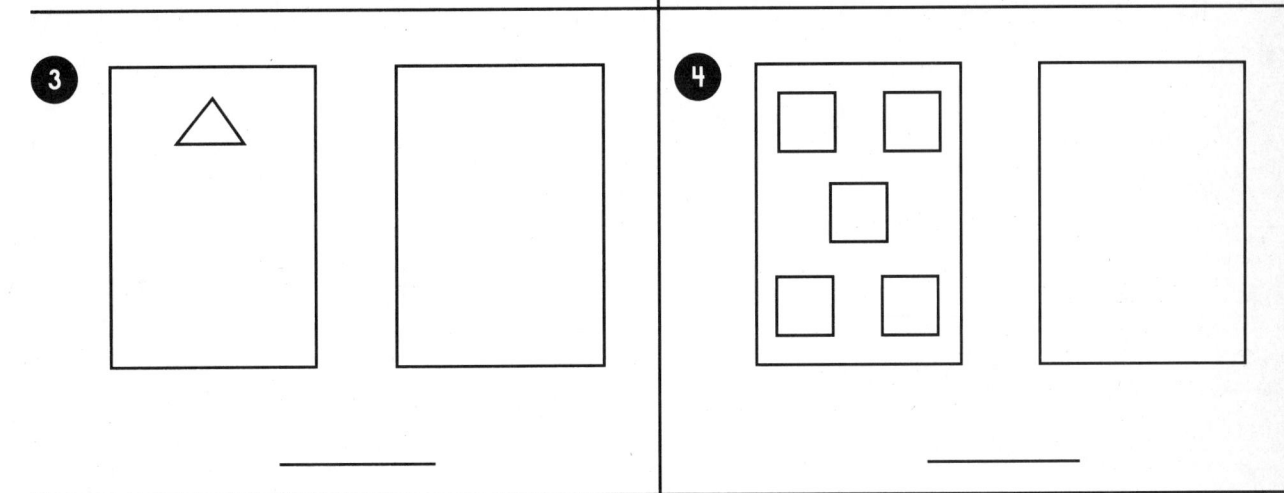

4)

_____

5)

_____

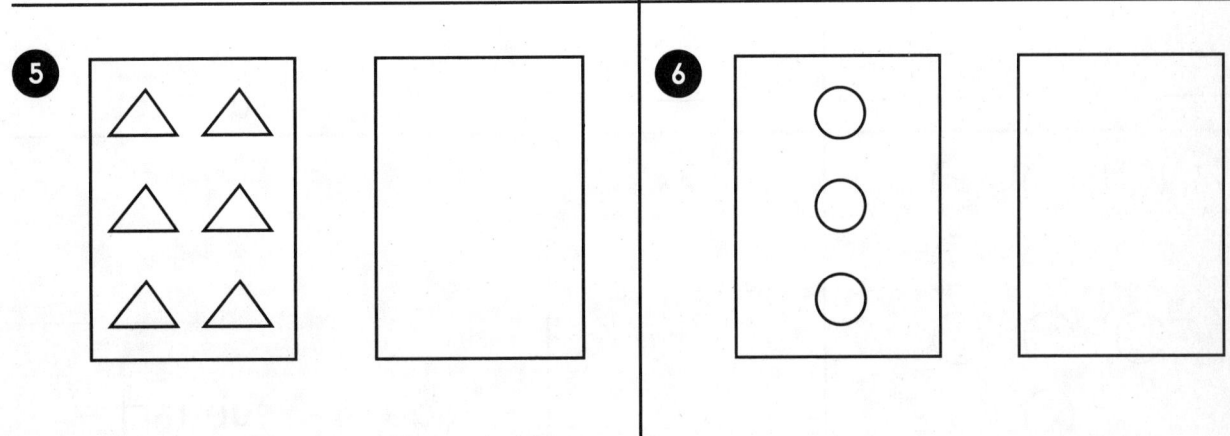

6)

_____

© Houghton Mifflin Company. All rights reserved/1

Module 2: Section A, Lesson 5

Name _____

Change the counters.
Draw the results.
Ring whether you add or subtract.

	Start with	Change to	Draw and ring.
1	○ ○ ○	5	add subtract
2	○ ○ ○ ○	1	add subtract
3	○ ○ ○ ○ ○ ○	9	add subtract
4	○ ○ ○ ○ ○ ○ ○ ○ ○ ○	2	add subtract

50   Module 2: Section A, Lesson 5   © Houghton Mifflin Company. All rights reserved/1

Name _____

Materials: Crayons

Draw a pattern on the first object.
Copy the pattern onto the second object.

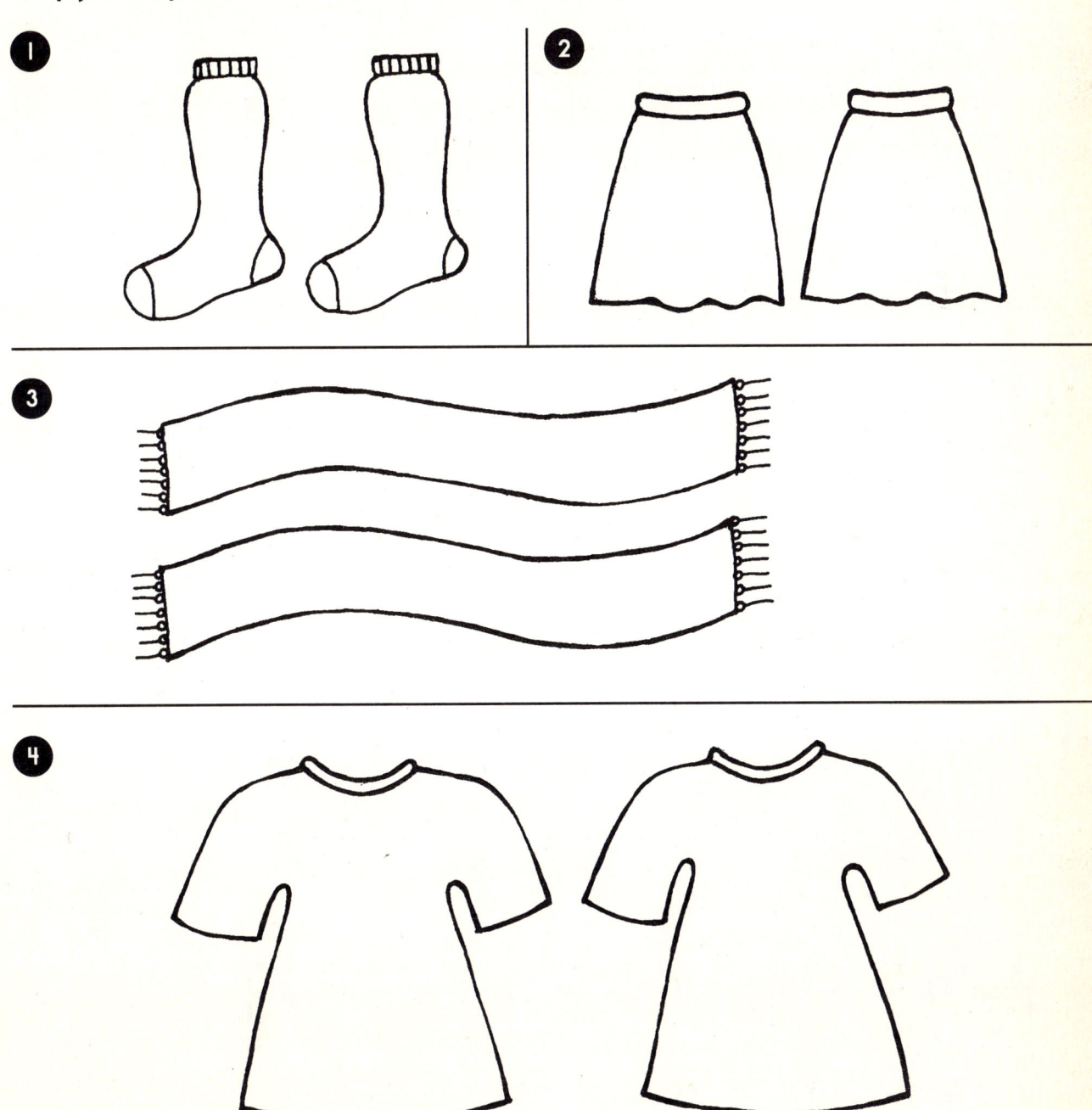

1.

2.

3.

4.

© Houghton Mifflin Company. All rights reserved/1

Module 2: Section B, Lesson 6   51

Name _____

Materials: Crayons

Color the pattern.
Then continue the pattern.

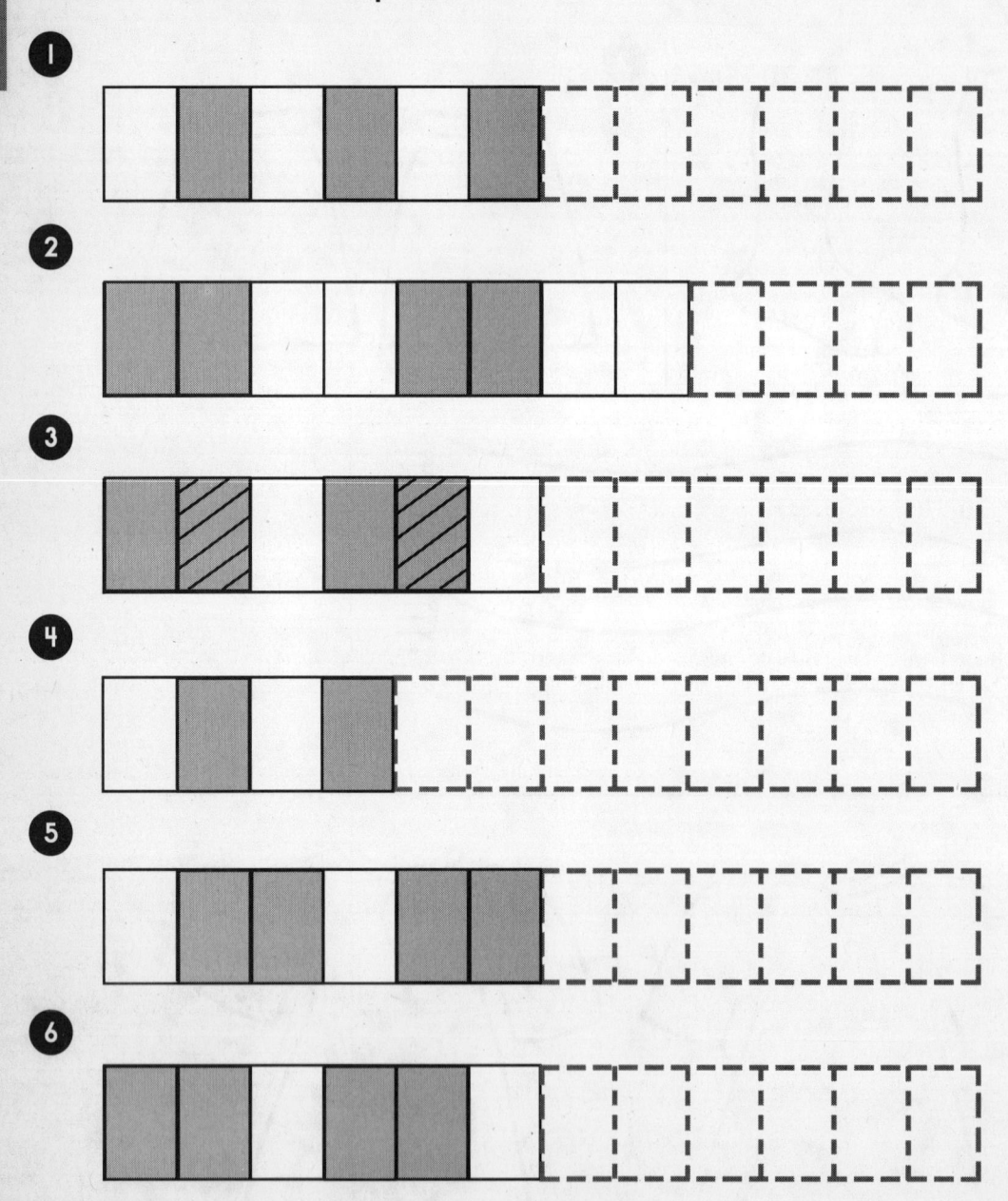

1.

2.

3.

4.

5.

6.

Underline the stem in each pattern.

52 Module 2: Section B, Lesson 7 © Houghton Mifflin Company. All rights reserved/1

Name _____

SKILL PLUS 27 WORKSHEET

Count.	Tally.	Write the number.
1	𝍷𝍷𝍷𝍷╱	_____
2		_____
3		_____

Draw.	Tally.	Write the number.
4	𝍷𝍷𝍷𝍷╱ 𝍷𝍷𝍷𝍷╱	_____
5	𝍷𝍷𝍷𝍷╱ 𝍷𝍷𝍷𝍷╱ |||	_____

© Houghton Mifflin Company. All rights reserved/1

Module 2: Section B, Lesson 8 53

Name _____

Draw the shapes in the ten-frames.
Write the number.

1

_____ in all

2

_____ in all

54   Module 2: Section B, Lesson 9

Name _____

Materials: Cubes

Estimate the length.
Then measure with cubes.

Estimate.   Measure.

1.

_____   _____

2.

_____   _____

3.

_____   _____

4.

_____   _____

© Houghton Mifflin Company. All rights reserved/1   Module 2: Section B, Lesson 10

Name _____

one 1 •
two 2 • •
three 3 • • •
four 4 • • • •
five 5 • • • • •

Draw the number of dots.	Write the number.	Write the number word.
1) 2		
2) 5		
3) 1		
4) 3		
5) 4		

Name _____

Materials: Crayons

six	seven	eight	nine	ten
6	7	8	9	10

Color parts that show 10 red.
Color parts that show less than 10 brown.
Color parts that show more than 10 yellow.

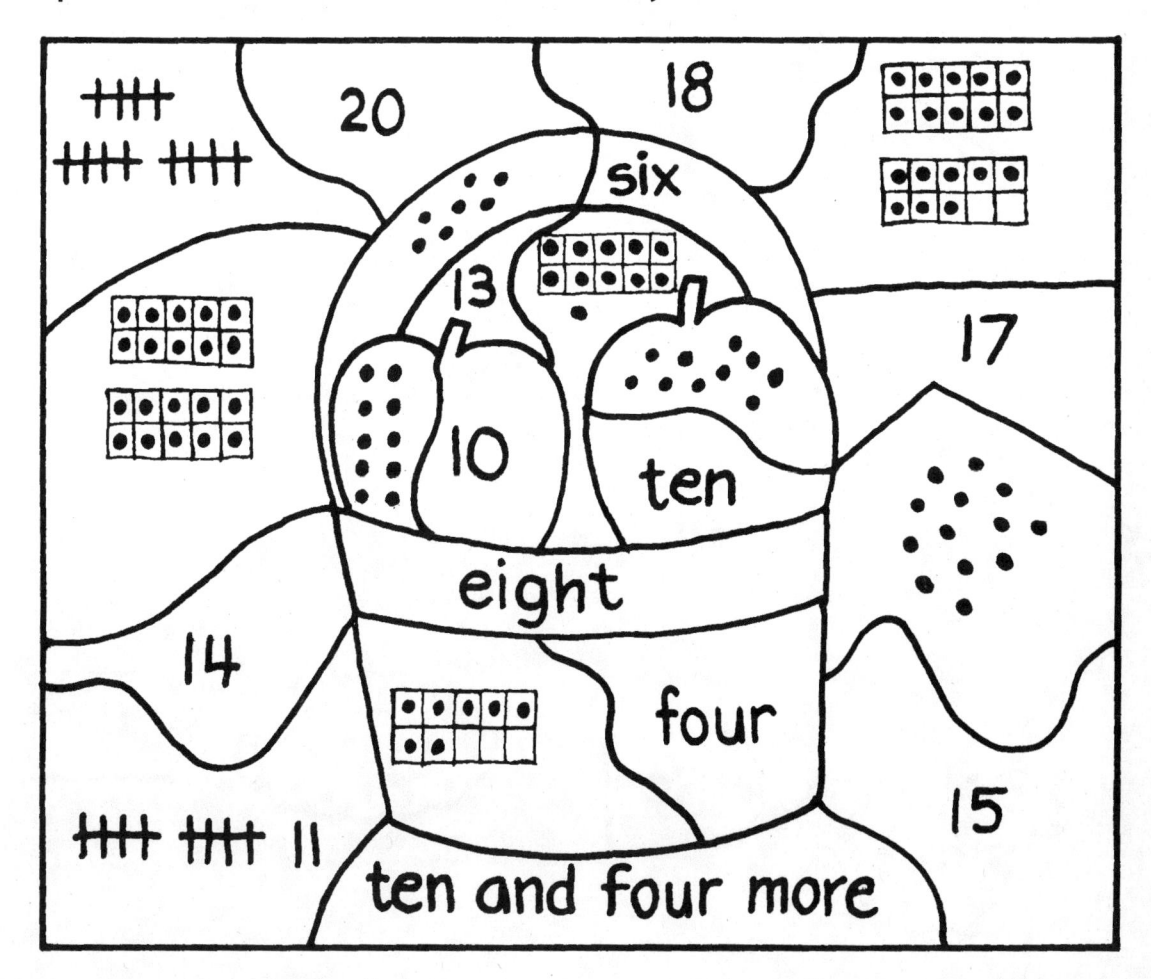

Module 2: Section C, Lesson 12   57

Name _____

Materials: Ten pennies, crayons

You have

What can you buy to spend all your money?
Color what you buy.

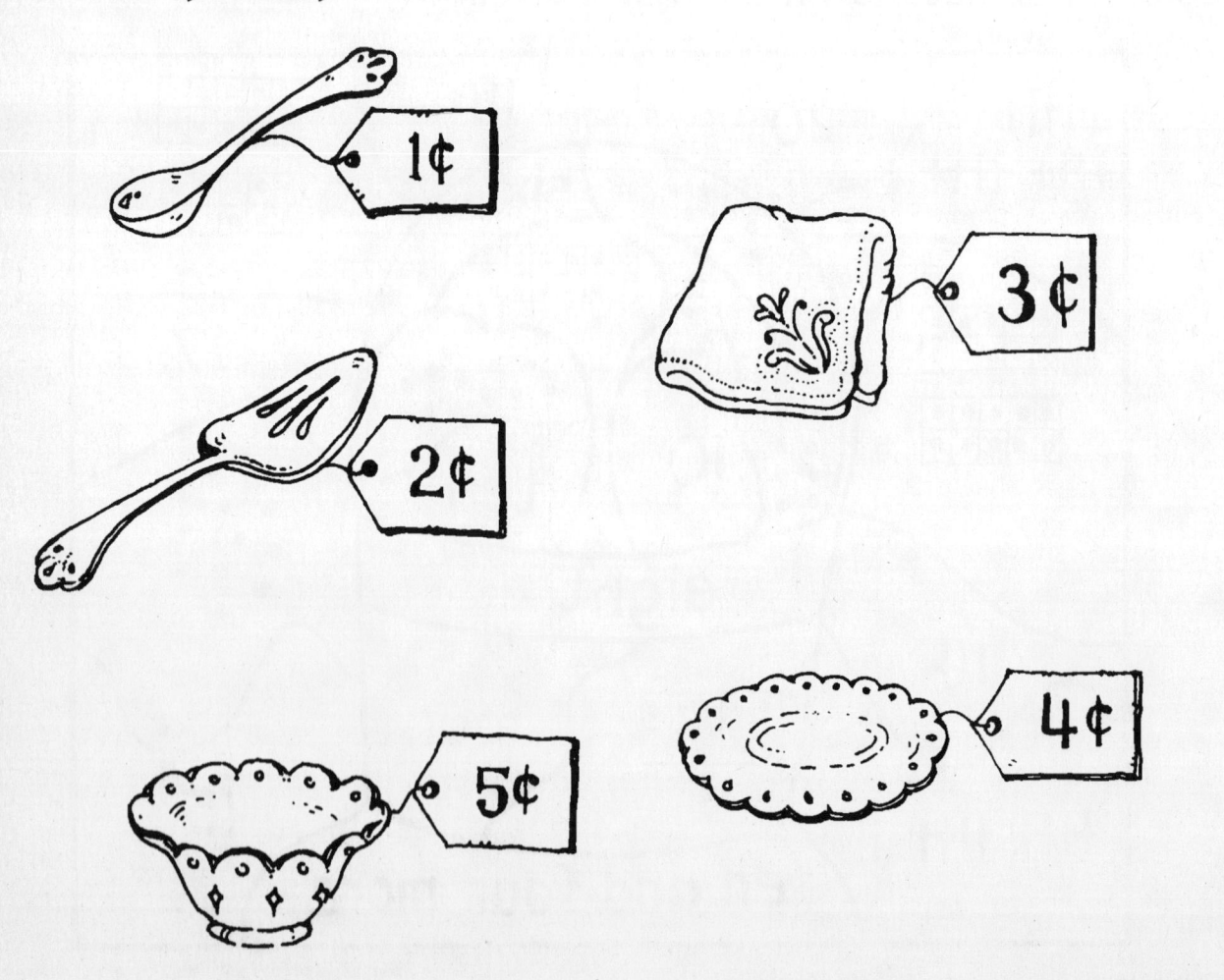

1¢

3¢

2¢

5¢

4¢

58   Module 2: Section C, Lesson 13   © Houghton Mifflin Company. All rights reserved/1

Name _____

Ring groups of ten.
Count the tens.

1

_____ tens

2

_____ tens

Name _____

SKILL PLUS 34 WORKSHEET

Materials: Markers and counters

Play with a partner. Take turns.
Move markers from home to the store.
One player moves to each shaded space.
The other player moves to each white space.
Say the numbers you land on.
Use counters to show numbers with rings.

Play again going from the store back to home.

60 Module 2: Section C, Lesson 15   © Houghton Mifflin Company. All rights reserved/1

Name _____

Write the numbers.

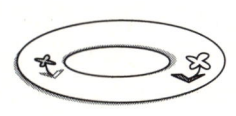

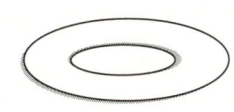

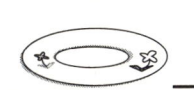

1

How many plates are there in all? ____

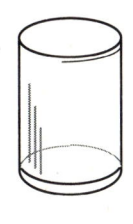

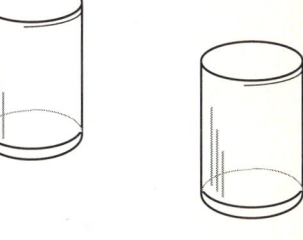

____   ____

2

How many glasses and cups are there in all? ____

____   ____

Draw some bowls and spoons.

3

bowls ____   spoons ____   How many bowls and spoons are there in all? ____

Module 3: Section A, Lesson 1

Name _____

Materials: Crayons

Think of a story about adding.
Ring the number sentence.
Color the pictures.

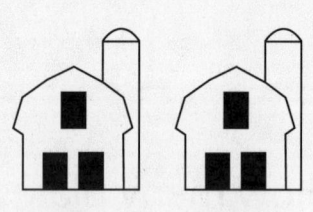

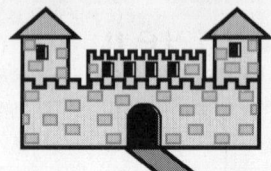

1

2 + 1 = 3

4 + 1 = 5

2

1 + 3 = 4

3 + 3 = 6

3

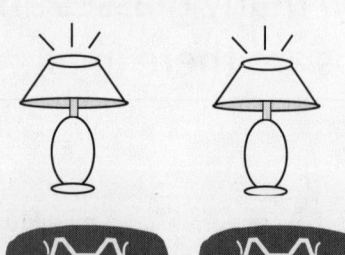

2 + 2 = 4

5 + 1 = 6

4

2 + 3 = 5

1 + 2 = 3

Name _____

**Draw groups that have more and less.
Then draw a group that is equal to the first.**

	More	Less	Equal to
1			
2			
3			
4			

© Houghton Mifflin Company. All rights reserved/1

Module 3: Section A, Lesson 2   63

Name _____

Materials: Counters

Use more counters.
Make equal groups.
Draw the new counters.

1. ○ ○ ○ ○ ○ = ○

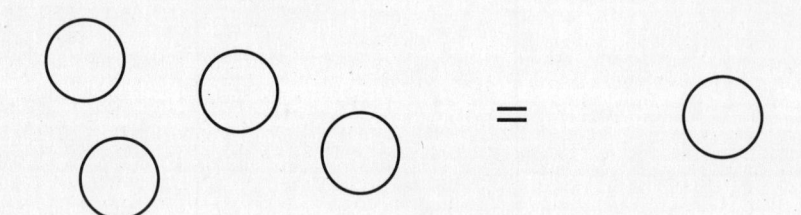

2. ○ ○ = ○ ○ ○ ○

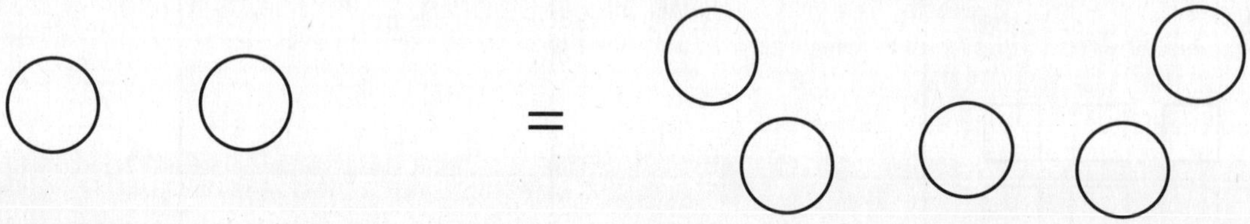

3. ○ ○ ○ = ○ ○

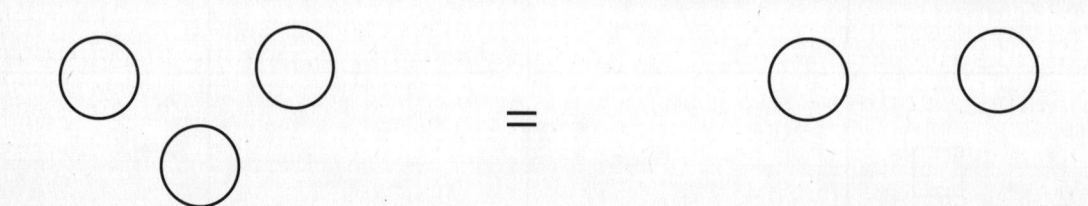

4. ○ ○ ○ ○ ○ ○ = ○ ○ ○ ○

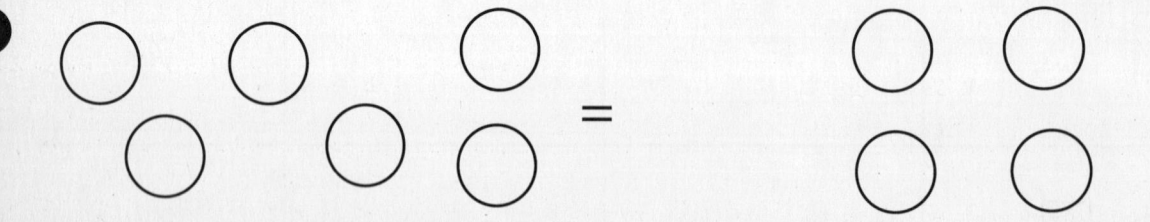

5. ○ ○ ○ = ○ ○ ○ ○ ○

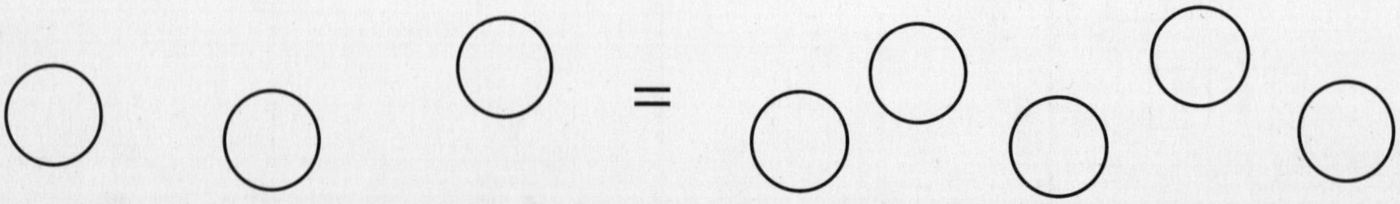

64 Module 3: Section A, Lesson 3 © Houghton Mifflin Company. All rights reserved/1

Name _____

Count on.
Complete the number sentence.

1.

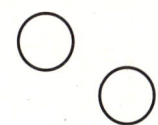

5 + 2 = ____

2.

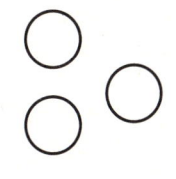

4 + ____ = ____

3.

____ + ____ = ____

4. Write and draw your own.

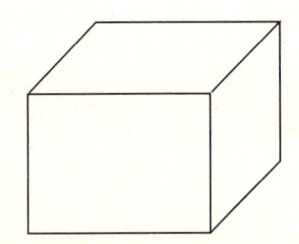

____ + ____ = ____

© Houghton Mifflin Company. All rights reserved/1   Module 3: Section A, Lesson 4

Name _____

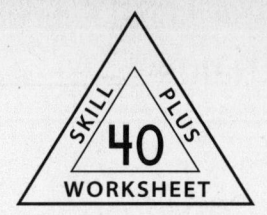

Complete the number sentence.

1

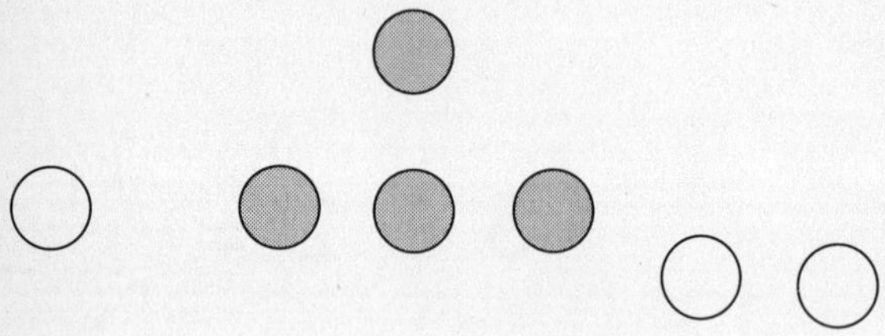

1 + 4 + 2 = _____

2

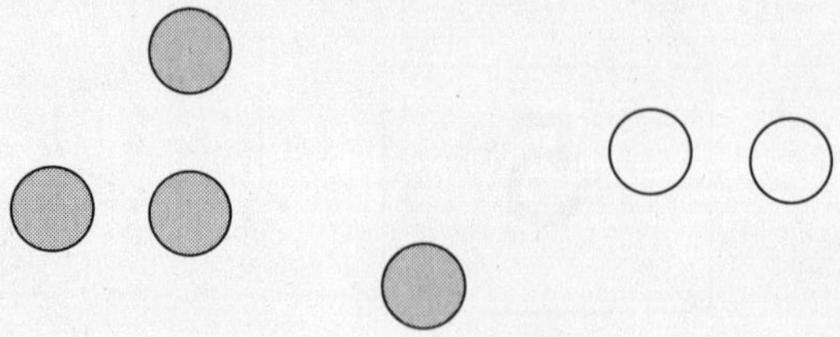

3 + 1 + 2 = _____

3

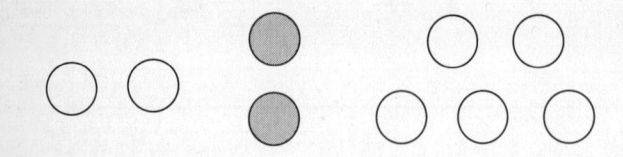

2 + 2 + 5 = _____

4

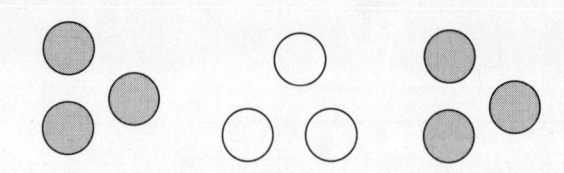

3 + 3 + 3 = _____

5 Draw and write your own.

_____ + _____ + _____ = _____

Name _____

SKILL PLUS 41 WORKSHEET

Draw the whole.
Then write the whole as a number.

	Part	Part	Whole	Number
1	○○○	○○○		_____
2	○○○	○		_____
3	5	2		_____
4	4	4		_____
5	4	0		_____

© Houghton Mifflin Company. All rights reserved/1   Module 3: Section A, Lesson 6

Name _____

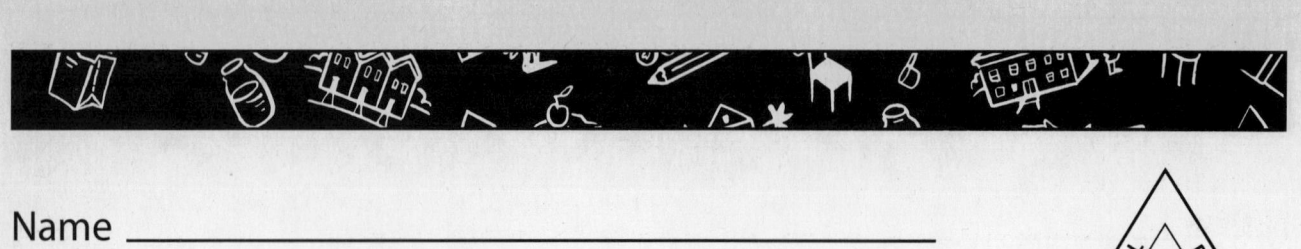

Materials: Pennies

Measure the length in pennies.

1

about _____ pennies

2

about _____ pennies

3

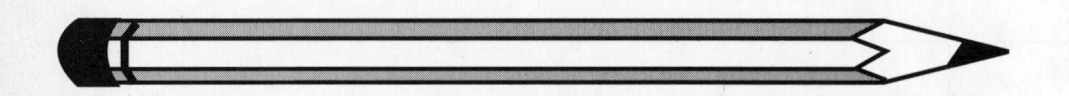

about _____ pennies

4

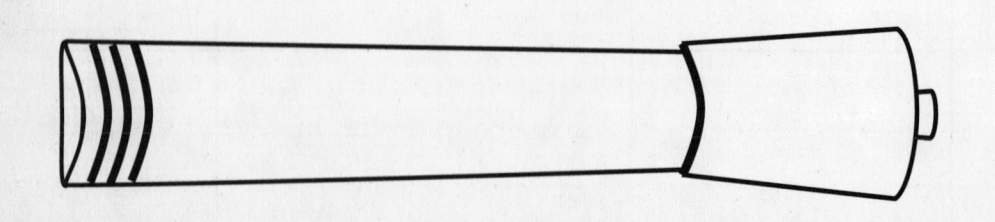

about _____ pennies

68 Module 3: Section B, Lesson 7

Name _____

Materials: Counters

Put the counters in the ten-frames.

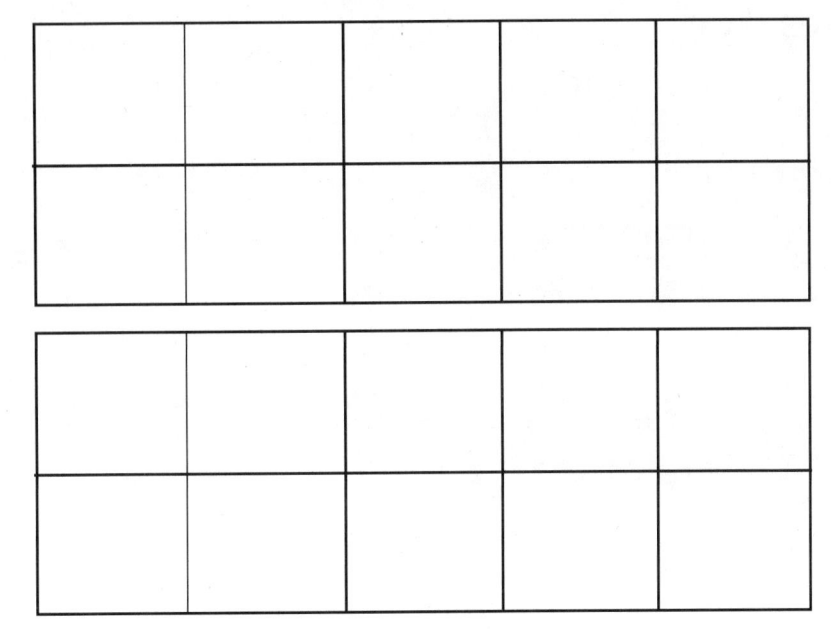

Start with	Add 1. Draw what you have.	Write the number.
❶ 11		_____
❷ 15		_____
❸ 18		_____
❹ 14		_____

Module 3: Section B, Lesson 8

Name _____

Materials: Crayons and cubes

Make a train to match the addition.
Color the boxes. Add.
Turn the train. Color and add.

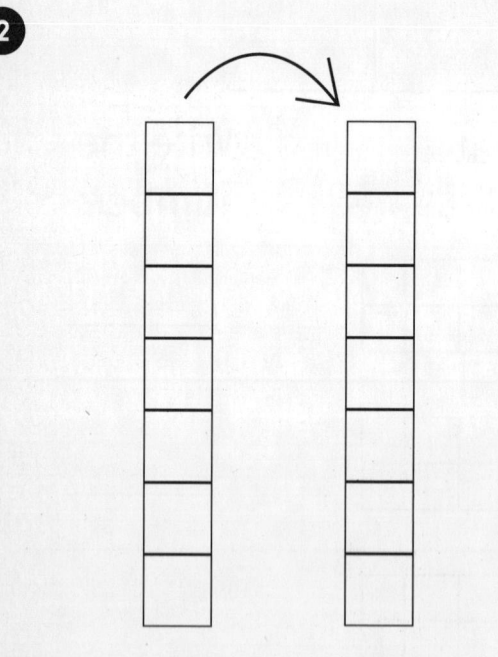

1

6 + 2 = _____

2 + 6 = _____

2   **3**

3   4   5   1
+4 +3   +1 +5

70   Module 3: Section B, Lesson 8

Name _____

Ring the one that holds more.

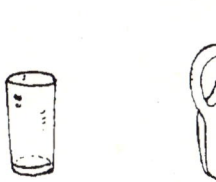

1

2

Ring the one that holds less.

3

4

Draw one that holds more.

5

Draw one that holds less.

6

Name _____

Materials: Cubes and crayons

Measure the ribbons in cubes.
Write the measurements.
Color.

① _____ cubes

② _____ cubes

③ _____ cubes

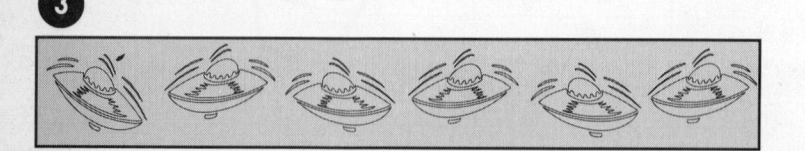

④ _____ cubes

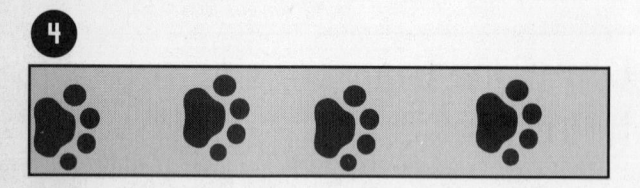

⑤ _____ cubes

72 Module 3: Section B, Lesson 10

Name _____

Draw the objects where they belong.
Draw **2** more objects of your own.

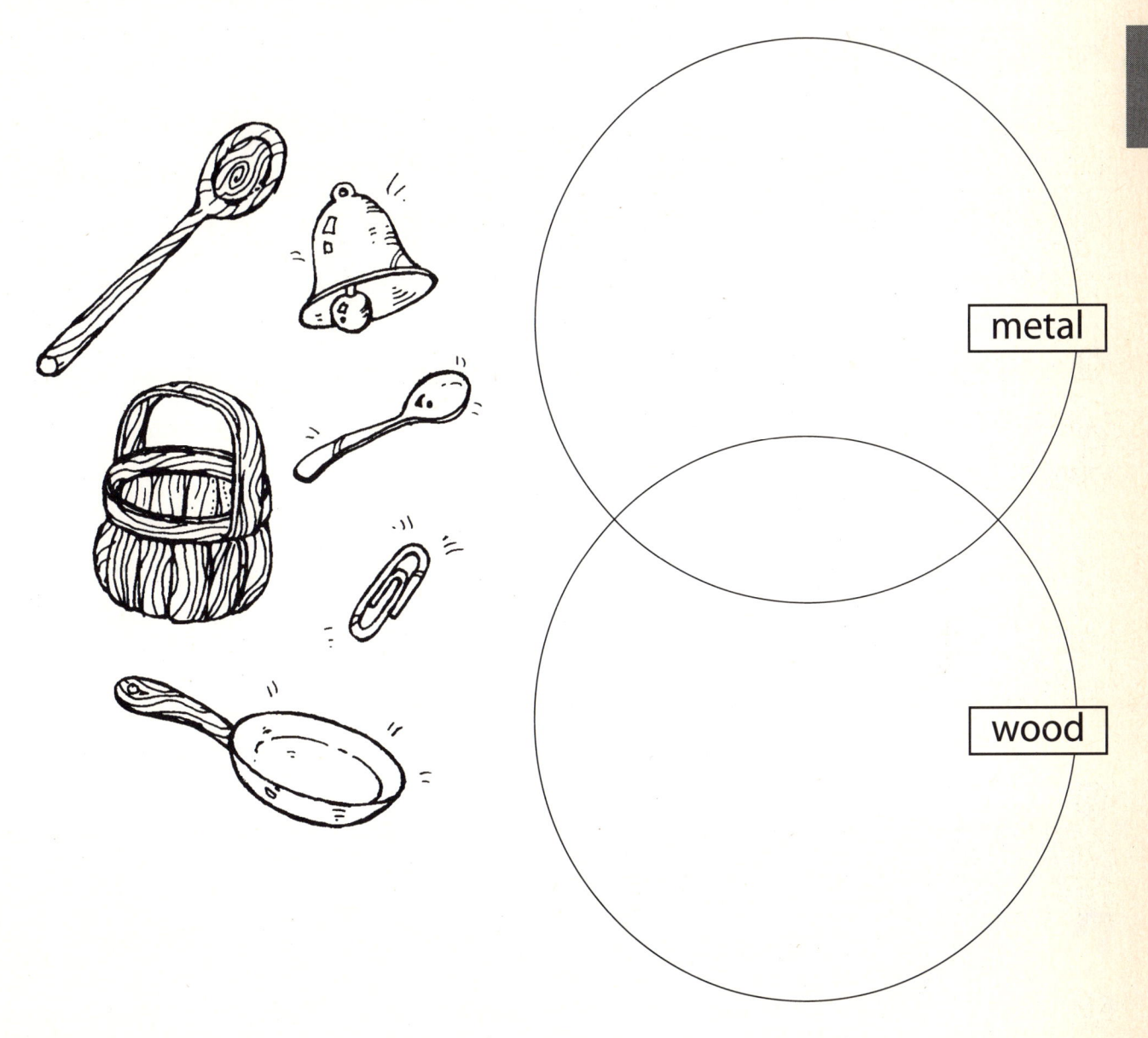

metal

wood

Module 3: Section C, Lesson 11

Name _____

Think of a story.
Complete the number sentences.

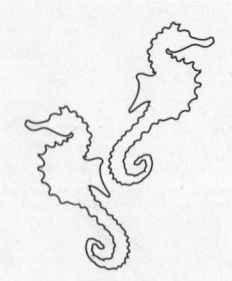

1

2 + 3 = ___   3 + 2 = ___

2

3 + 4 = ___   ___ + ___ = ___

Think of a story. Draw.
Complete the number sentences.

3

___ + ___ = ___   ___ + ___ = ___

74 Module 3: Section C, Lesson 12

Name _____

Materials: Crayons

Color the animals.

Estimate the number. Then count.

Did you make a good guess? Color the face.

Estimate.   Count.

1. 🐖 _____   _____   😊 😟
2. 🐑 _____   _____   😊 😟
3. 🐓 _____   _____   😊 😟
4. 🐔 _____   _____   😊 😟

© Houghton Mifflin Company. All rights reserved/1

Module 3: Section C, Lesson 13   75

Name _____

Draw what comes out of the machine.

1. Add 2.

2. Add 1.

3. Add 3.

4. Add 5.

5. Add 2.

6. Add 4.

76 Module 3: Section C, Lesson 14   © Houghton Mifflin Company. All rights reserved/1

Name _____

Materials: Crayons

Which clown is it?
Use the clues.
Draw the answer. Color.

① has dots
has flower
has pointed hat

② has stripes
is tall
has flower

③ has stripes
is short
has rope

④ has flower
has dots
has curly hair

© Houghton Mifflin Company. All rights reserved/1

Module 3: Section C, Lesson 15   77

Name _____

Materials: Crayons

Color ▭ yellow.

Color △ brown.

Color ▯ red.

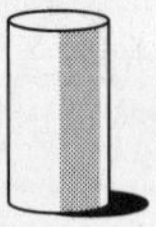

Color ◯ blue.

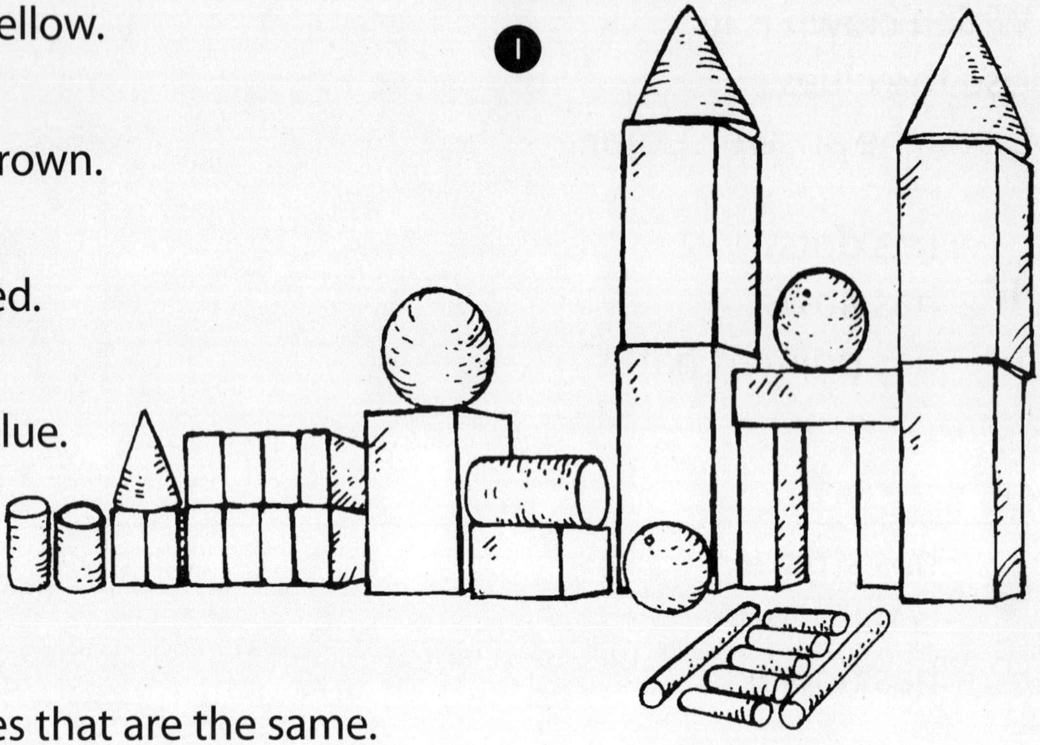

Match shapes that are the same.
Color.

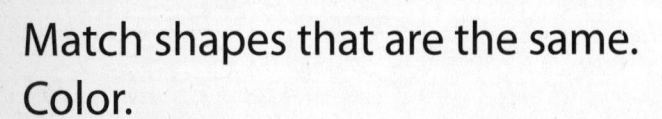

2.

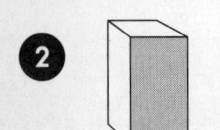

3.

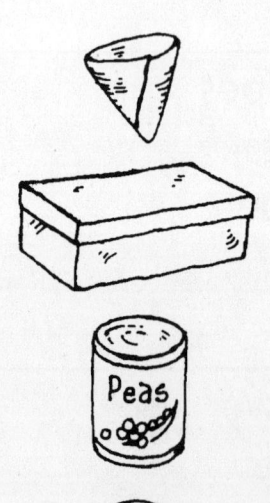

4.

5.

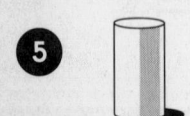

78 Module 4: Section A, Lesson 1   © Houghton Mifflin Company. All rights reserved/1

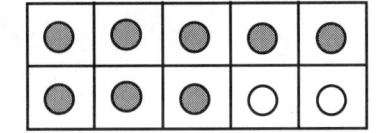

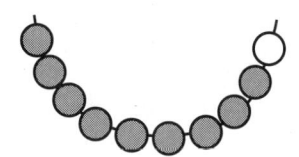

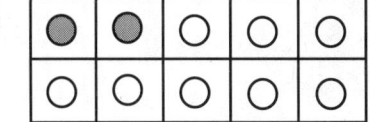

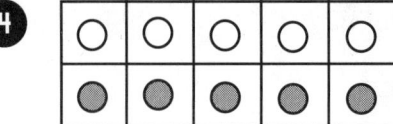

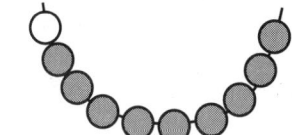

Name _____

Materials: Crayons

Write different ways to make 10.
Color.

1.

    6 + _____

2.

    2 + _____

3.

    ___ + ___

4.

    ___ + ___

5.

    ___ + ___

6.

    ___ + ___

7.

    ___ + ___

8.

    ___ + ___

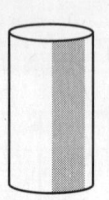

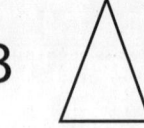

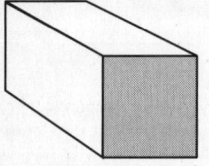

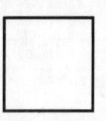

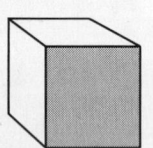

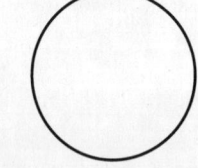

Name _____

Materials: Crayons

Match the shape to its bottom face.

1. (cone) A ○

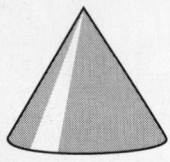

2. (cylinder) B △

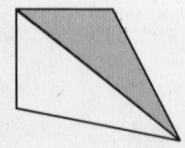

3. (rectangular prism) C ☐

4. (cube) D ◯

5. (triangular pyramid) E ▯

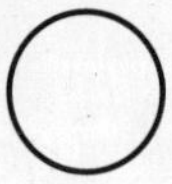

80   Module 4: Section A, Lesson 3   © Houghton Mifflin Company. All rights reserved/1

Name _____

Materials: Counters

Add on with counters.
Write the number you get.

	Start With	Add On	Numbers You Have
❶	○ ○	3	_____
❷	○ ○ ○ ○ ○ ○	2	_____
❸	8	1	_____
❹	7	3	_____
❺	5	2	_____

Make your own.
Write the numbers.

❻ _____ | _____ | _____

© Houghton Mifflin Company. All rights reserved/1

Module 4: Section A, Lesson 4 81

Name _____

Think of stories about taking away.
Write how many are left.

1. ○ ○ ○ ⊗ ⊗ ⊗ ____

2. △ △ △ △ △ △ ✕ ✕ ____

3. ☐ ☐ ☐ ☐ ☐ ☐ ☐ ⊠ ____

4. ▭ ▭ ⊠ ▭ ▭ ⊠ ____

5. Draw one of your own.

____

82 Module 4: Section A, Lesson 4   © Houghton Mifflin Company. All rights reserved/1

Name _____

Materials: Crayons

Draw each shape in the table.

Use the table to solve.

① How many ▭ are there? _____

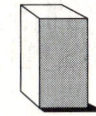

② How many △ are there? _____

③ Which shape has **3** objects? _____

④ Which shape has the fewest objects? _____

© Houghton Mifflin Company. All rights reserved/1

Module 4: Section A, Lesson 5   83

Name _____

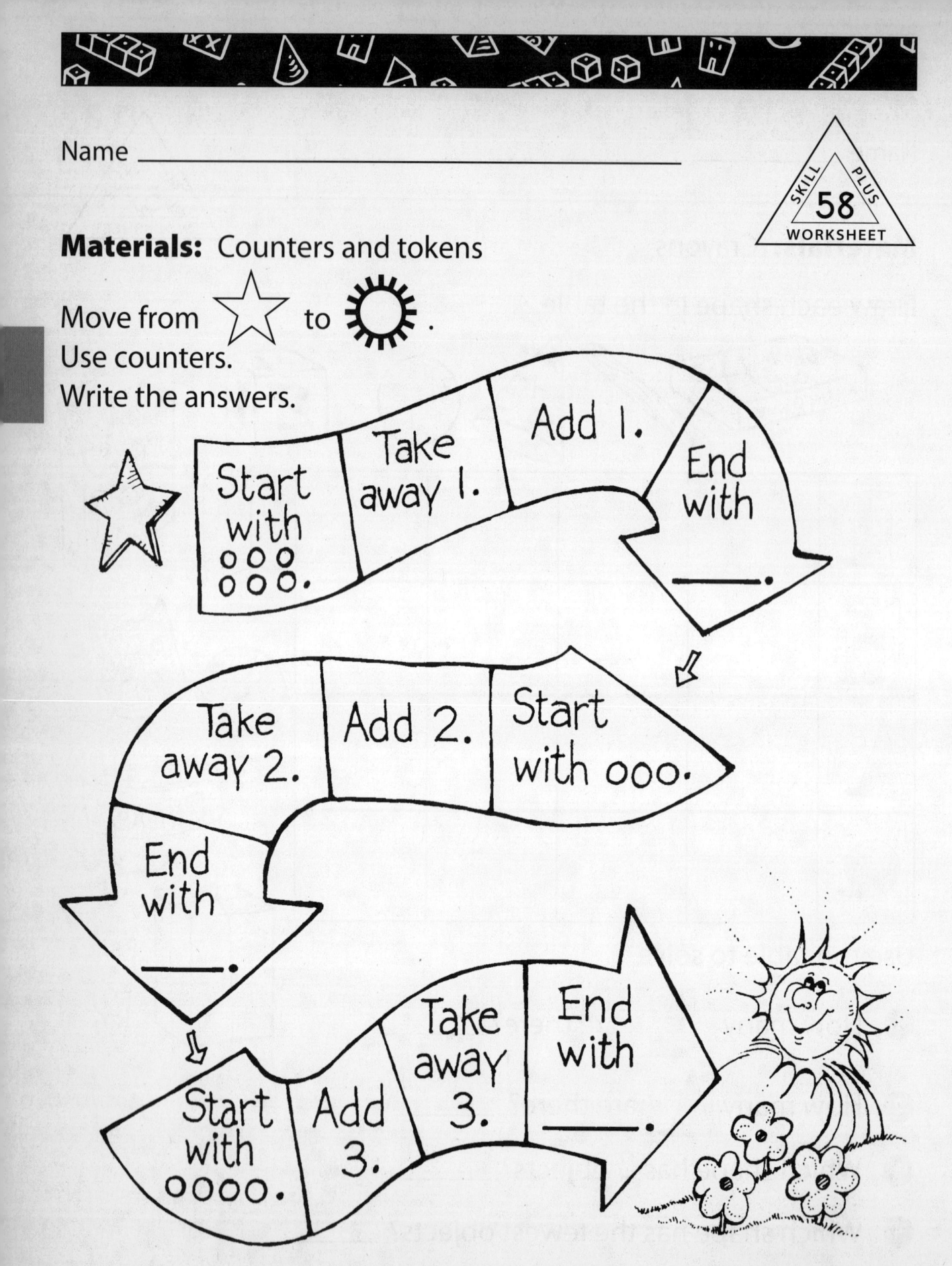

Materials: Counters and tokens

Move from ☆ to ☼.
Use counters.
Write the answers.

Start with ooo ooo. → Take away 1. → Add 1. → End with ___.

Start with ooo. → Add 2. → Take away 2. → End with ___.

Start with oooo. → Add 3. → Take away 3. → End with ___.

84 Module 4: Section B, Lesson 6 © Houghton Mifflin Company. All rights reserved/1

Name _____

Materials: Counters

Use counters to act out.
Write the answers.

1 There are **8** counters in all.

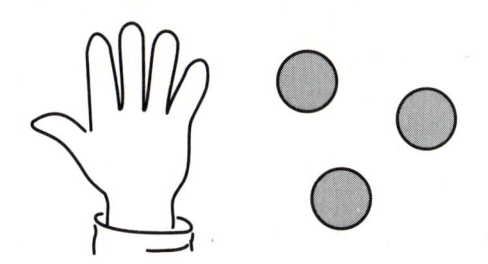

How many counters
are under the hand? _____

2 There are **6** stars in all.

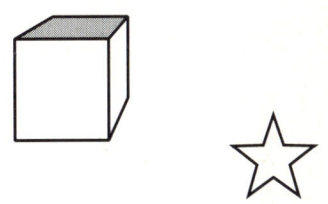

How many stars
are in the box? _____

3 There are **4** counters in all.

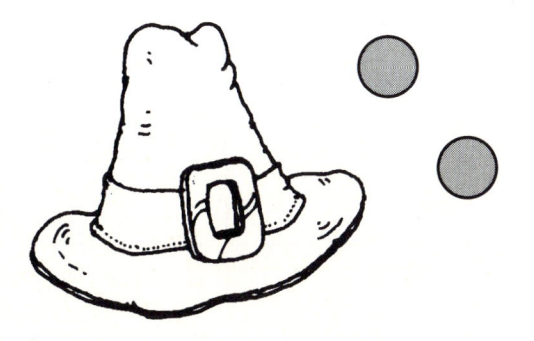

How many counters
are under the hat? _____

4 There are **7** counters in all.

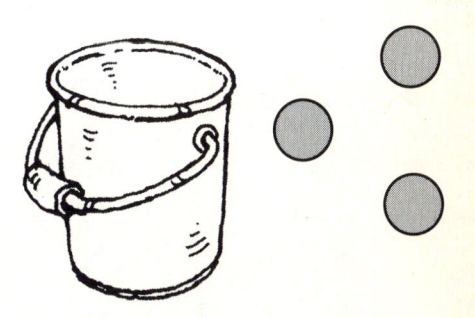

How many counters
are in the bucket? _____

Name _____

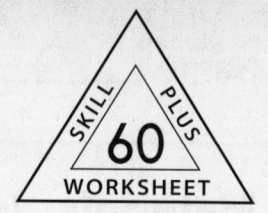

Materials: Pennies

How many pennies do you need?
Act out the problem. Write the amount.

	Pennies You Have	What You Want to Buy	Pennies You Need
1	(3 pennies)	flower pot 10¢	_____ ¢
2	(6 pennies)	SEEDS 6¢	_____ ¢
3	(2 pennies)	watering can 7¢	_____ ¢
4	(6 pennies)	shovel 10¢	_____ ¢

86 Module 4: Section B, Lesson 8   © Houghton Mifflin Company. All rights reserved/1

Name _____

Materials: Pennies

Use pennies to buy two. Act it out.

5¢   7¢   3¢   2¢   9¢

Buy.	Count pennies. Then draw.	What do you spend?
❶ (muffin, banana)		_____ ¢
❷ (donut, muffin)		_____ ¢
❸ (milk, juice box)		_____ ¢
❹ Draw your own.		_____ ¢

SKILL PLUS 61 WORKSHEET

© Houghton Mifflin Company. All rights reserved/1   Module 4: Section B, Lesson 9   87

Name _____

Materials: Crayons

Think of a subtraction story.
Draw a picture. Write and solve.

1

_____ − _____ = _____

2

_____ − _____ = _____

3

_____ − _____ = _____

Name _____

SKILL PLUS 63 WORKSHEET

Materials: Cubes and red, blue, and yellow crayons

Make a train with **5** cubes.
Color longer strings red.
Color shorter strings blue.
Color strings the same length yellow.

1. 〰️
2. 〰️〰️〰️
3. 〰️〰️〰️〰️
4. 〰️
5. 〰️〰️〰️〰️〰️
6. 〰️〰️
7. 〰️

Ring the longest and the shortest strings.

© Houghton Mifflin Company. All rights reserved/1   Module 4: Section C, Lesson 11   89

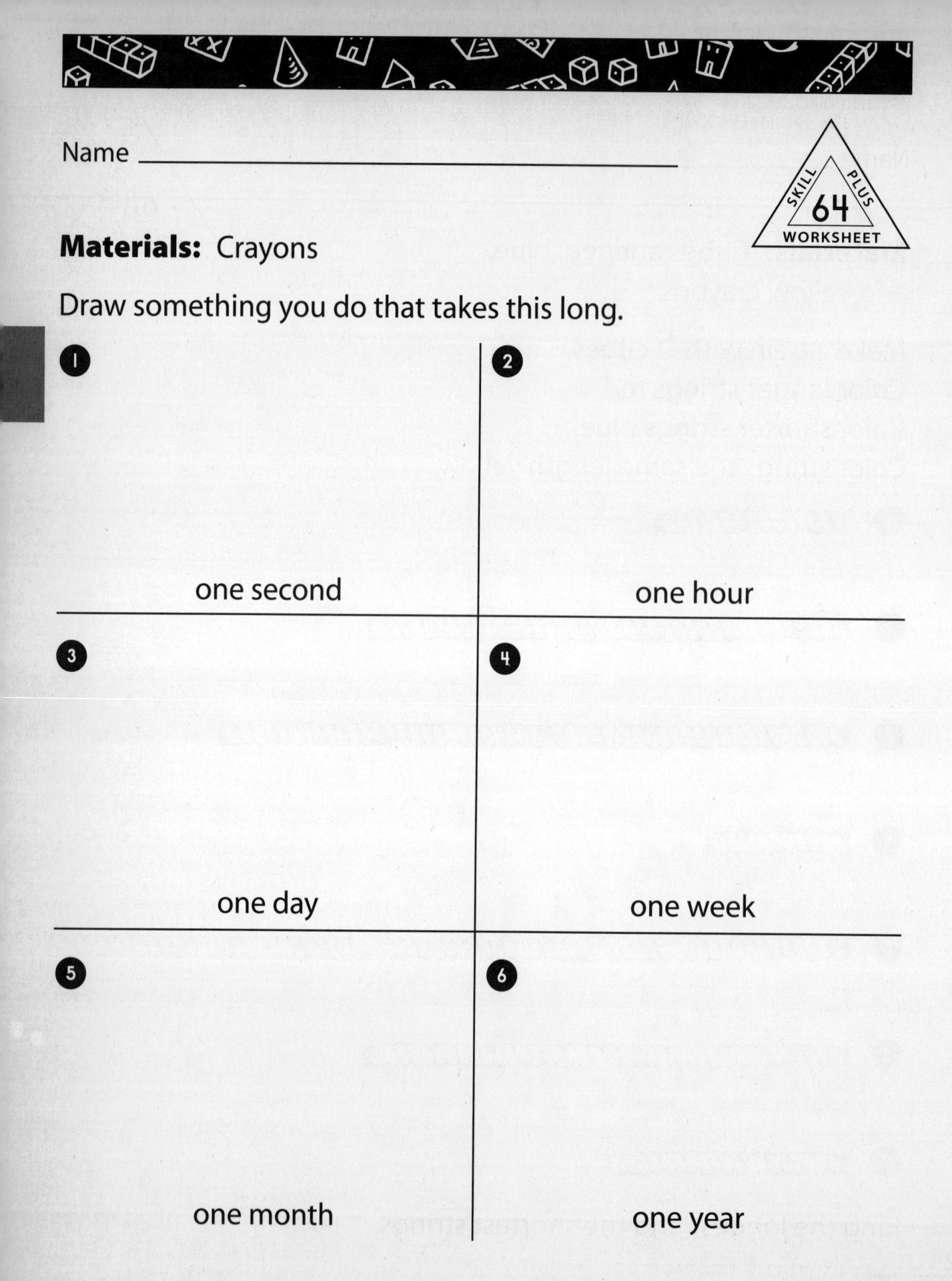

Name _____

SKILL PLUS WORKSHEET 64

Materials: Crayons

Draw something you do that takes this long.

1

one second

2

one hour

3

one day

4

one week

5

one month

6

one year

90   Module 4: Section C, Lesson 12   © Houghton Mifflin Company. All rights reserved/1

Name _____

Materials: Crayons

How long does it take?
Ring the best estimate. Color.

1 lace a shoe

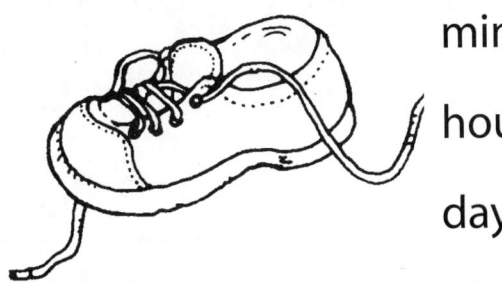

minutes
hours
days

2 plant a garden

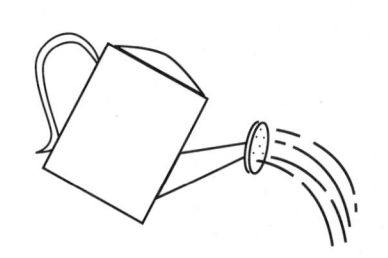

minutes
hours
days

3 paint a house

minutes
hours
days

4 watch a play

minutes
hours
days

5 make a sandwich

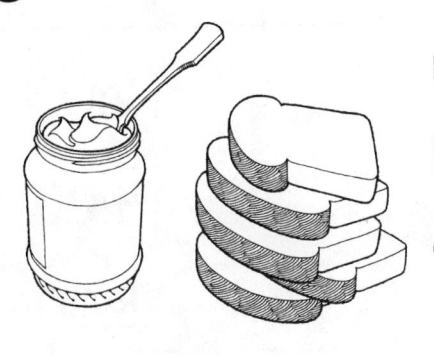

minutes
hours
days

6 read a book

minutes
hours
days

Name _____

Materials: Crayons

What time is it? Draw a picture.
Ring your estimate.

1 breakfast time

7:00

11:00

2:00

2 lunch time

12:00

5:00

8:00

3 after school fun

4:00

9:00

11:00

4 bedtime story

12:00

4:00

8:00

92 Module 4: Section C, Lesson 14 © Houghton Mifflin Company. All rights reserved/1

Name _____

Materials: Cubes

Trace around your hand.
Estimate and measure.

SKILL PLUS 67 WORKSHEET

① estimate _____
measure _____

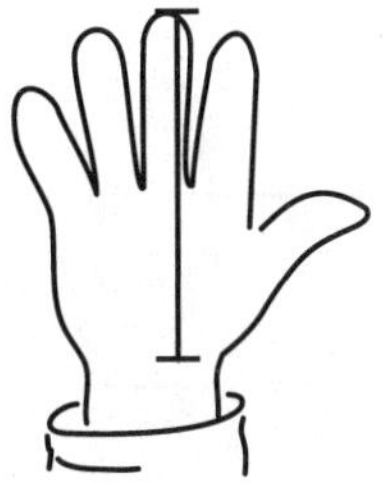

② estimate _____
measure _____

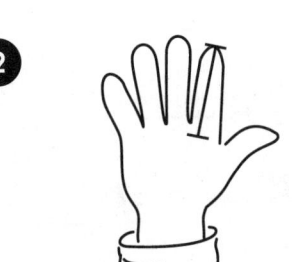

③ estimate _____
measure _____

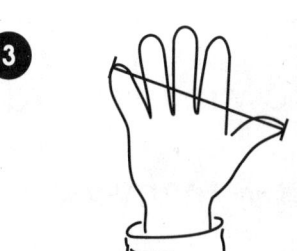

© Houghton Mifflin Company. All rights reserved/1

Module 4: Section C, Lesson 15

Name _____

Write the letters of the words in the graph.

words   say   graph   count   draw

Useful Words

0   1   2   3   4   5   6

Solve.

① Which words have 5 letters? _____
_____

② How many words have 3 letters? _____

③ How many words have 4 letters? _____

④ Write a sentence about the graph. _____
_____
_____

94 Module 5: Section A, Lesson 1   © Houghton Mifflin Company. All rights reserved/1

Name _____

Materials: Crayons

Draw pictures.
Write the answers.

1 Start with 6.
Subtract 4.

How many
are left? _____

2 Start with 3.
Subtract 1.
Add 1.

How many
are there now? _____

3 Start with 5.
Add 2.
Subtract 2.

How many
are there now? _____

4 Start with _____.

Subtract _____.

How many
are left? _____

Name _____

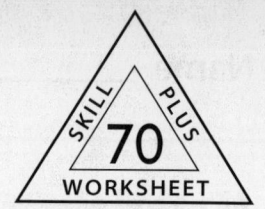

Think of a story about subtraction.
Cover some.
Write the number left.

Number Left

1.

2.

3.

4.

96 Module 5: Section A, Lesson 3

© Houghton Mifflin Company. All rights reserved/1

Name _____

Materials: Crayons

Ring the number sentence that tells the story.
Color.

1

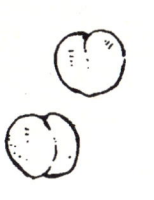

2 + 3 = 5
1 − 3 = 4

2

4 − 1 = 3
5 − 4 = 1

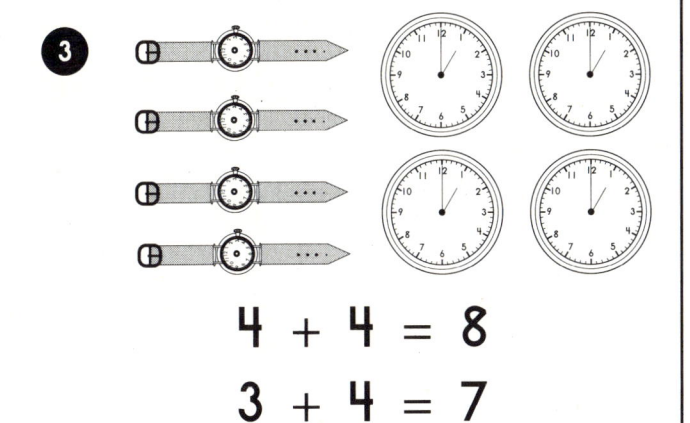

3

4 + 4 = 8
3 + 4 = 7

4

4 + 2 = 6
3 − 1 = 2

Draw a picture to match the number sentence

5

5 − 3 = 2

6

2 + 4 = 6

© Houghton Mifflin Company. All rights reserved/1

Module 5: Section A, Lesson 4   97

Name _____

Read the graph.

Number of Letters

G	A	M	E	S
C	A	N		
B	E			
F	U	N		

0   1   2   3   4   5

Use the graph to solve.

1 Write two things that the graph shows.

_____

_____

2 Which word has 5 letters? _____

3 Which words have the same number of letters? _____

_____

4 Which word has the least number of letters? _____

5 Change FUN to FUNNY on the graph. How does the graph change? _____

98   Module 5: Section A, Lesson 4   © Houghton Mifflin Company. All rights reserved/1

Name _____

SKILL PLUS WORKSHEET 73

Draw the picture on the grid.
Start at 0 to find its place.

			Place across	up
1	STOP	sign	1	4
2	▲	tent	2	3
3	⛵	pond	5	1
4	🪑	picnic area	5	4
5		Your choice!	4	2

Module 5: Section A, Lesson 5

Name _____

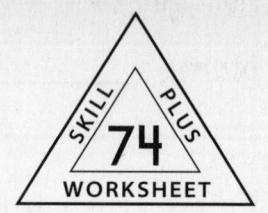

Materials: Counters

Move a stack of counters.
Follow the arrows.
Write the numbers.

Start with 5.	Add 2.	Subtract 1.	Subtract 1.
		I have ____.	I have ____.
	I have 7.		
Add 4.	Add 5.	Subtract 3.	Add 3.
I have ____.	I have ____.	I have ____.	I have ____.
Add 1.	Add 6.	Subtract 4.	Add 2.
I have ____.	I have ____.	I have ____.	I have ____.
Add 3.	Add 1.	Subtract 4.	Subtract 4.
I have ____.	I have ____.	I have ____.	I have ____.

100   Module 5: Section A, Lesson 6

Name _____

△ 75 SKILL PLUS WORKSHEET

Cross out to show subtraction.
Think about stories.

1

Subtract 4.

_____ are left.

2

Subtract 2.

_____ are left.

3

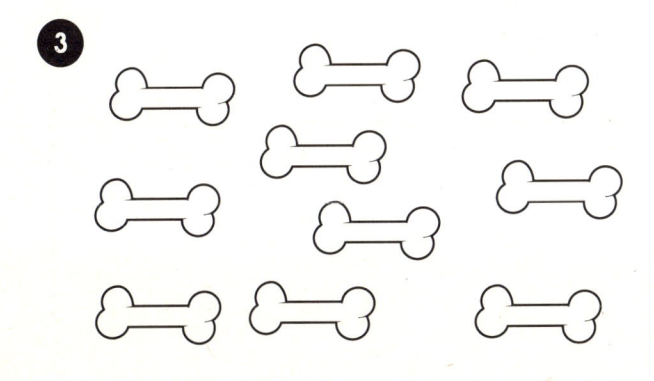

Subtract 7.

_____ are left.

4

Subtract _____.

_____ are left.

© Houghton Mifflin Company. All rights reserved/1

Module 5: Section B, Lesson 7   101

Name _____

SKILL PLUS WORKSHEET 76

Write how many objects went away.

	Once there were these.	Now there are these.	How many went away?
1	(8 gray circles)	(5 gray circles)	
2	(8 white circles)	(1 white circle)	
3	(8 black circles)	(3 black circles)	
4	(9 striped circles)	(3 striped circles)	

Draw your own.

5			

102   Module 5: Section B, Lesson 8   © Houghton Mifflin Company. All rights reserved/1

Name _____

Materials: Pennies

Use pennies. Act out the problems.
Write the answers.

1 You have **5** pennies.
You want to buy this.

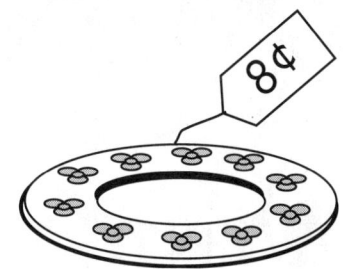

How many pennies
do you need?

_____ pennies

2 You have **10** pennies.
You spend **3¢**.

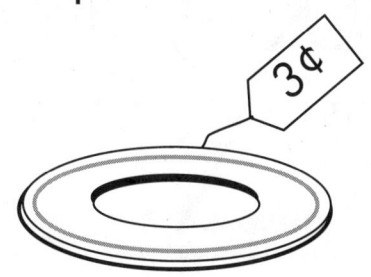

How many pennies
do you have left?

_____ pennies

3 You have **7¢** in all.

How many pennies
are you hiding?

_____ pennies

4 Write your own
subtraction problem.

_____

_____

_____

_____

_____

© Houghton Mifflin Company. All rights reserved/1

Module 5: Section B, Lesson 9   103

SKILL PLUS 77 WORKSHEET

Name _____

Materials: Crayons

Color green if the answer is **6**.
Color purple if the answer is **8** or more.
Color brown if answer if **5** or less.

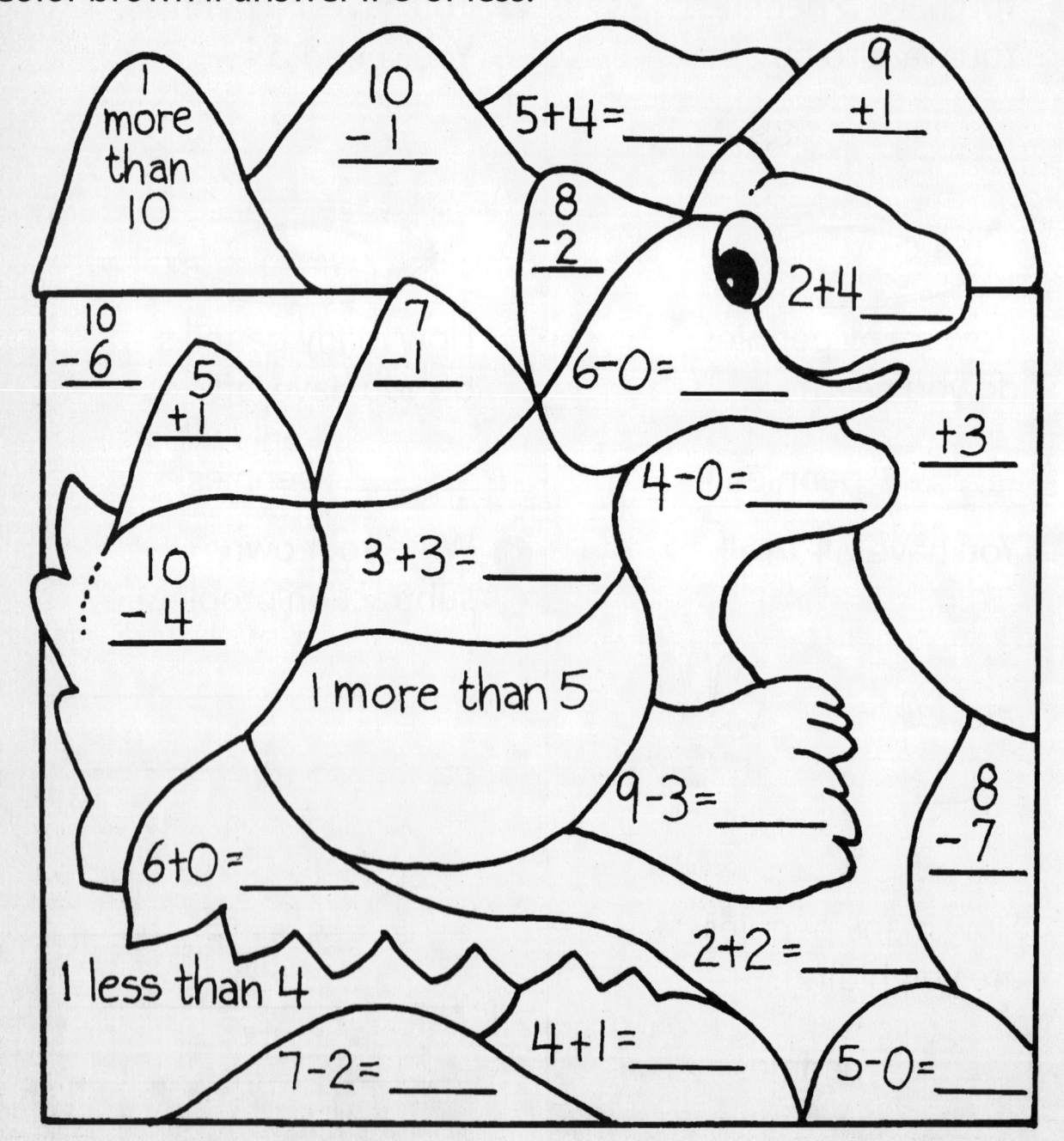

SKILL PLUS 78 WORKSHEET

1 more than 10

10 − 1

5 + 4 = ___

9 +1 ___

10 − 6

5 +1 ___

7 −1 ___

8 −2 ___

6 − 0 = ___

2 + 4 ___

1 +3 ___

10 − 4

3 + 3 = ___

4 − 0 = ___

1 more than 5

6 + 0 = ___

9 − 3 = ___

8 −7 ___

1 less than 4

2 + 2 = ___

7 − 2 = ___

4 + 1 = ___

5 − 0 = ___

104   Module 5: Section B, Lesson 10   © Houghton Mifflin Company. All rights reserved/1

Name _____

The amount changes.
Ring what happens.
Then write the number.

	From	To	Ring what happens.	How many did you add or subtract?
1	(7 circles)	(3 circles)	add / subtract	_____
2	(6 triangles)	(5 triangles)	add / subtract	_____
3	10	4	add / subtract	_____
4	2	6	add / subtract	_____

Try one of your own.

| 5 | | | add / subtract | _____ |

Module 5: Section C, Lesson 11   105

Name _____

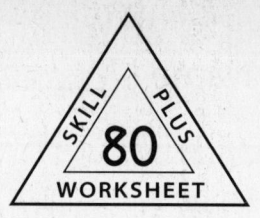

Materials: Crayons

Write the subtractions in their answers.

10 − 4
8 − 3
7 − 1
8 − 2
7 − 2
9 − 3
10 − 5
7 − 3
5 − 1
8 − 4
5 − 0
9 − 5

106 Module 5: Section C, Lesson 12

Name _____

Materials: Cubes

Show with cubes. Write the numbers.

	Make.	Remove.	Write.
1	[7 cubes]	2	7 − ___ = ___
2	[8 cubes]	6	___ − 6 = ___
3	[3 cubes]	3	___ − ___ = ___
4	[8 cubes]	___	___ − ___ = ___

Try your own.

	Make.	Remove.	Write.
5		___	___ − ___ = ___
6		___	___ − ___ = ___
7		___	___ − ___ = ___

Module 5: Section C, Lesson 13   107

Name _____

Materials: Crayons

Think about subtraction stories.
Write the subtraction two ways. Color.

1

[10]
− [ ]
———
[ ]

10 − ___ = ___

2

[ ]
− [ ]
———
[ ]

___ − ___ = ___

3

[ ]
− [ ]
———
[ ]

___ − ___ = ___

108 Module 5: Section C, Lesson 14

Name _____

Materials: Crayons

Match the number sentence to its picture.
Write the answer. Color.

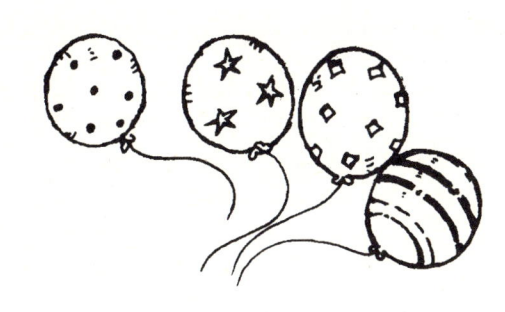

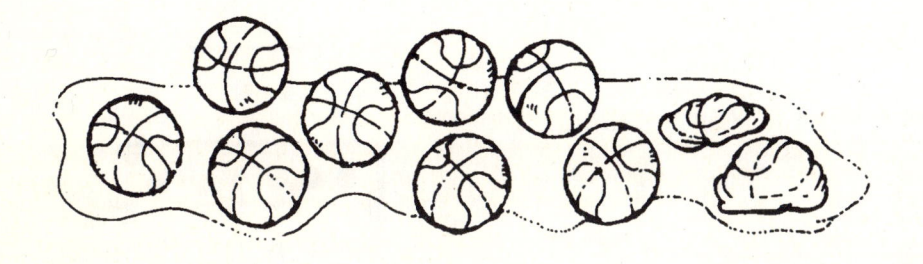

5 + 4 = ____

10 − 2 = ____

6 − 1 = ____

7 − 3 = ____

Name _____

Ring the doubles cards.
Match the number sentences to their cards.
Write the answers.

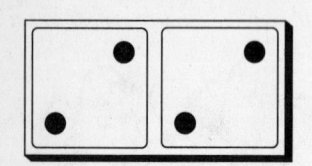

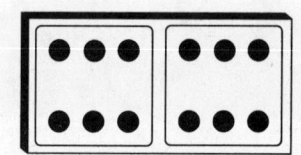

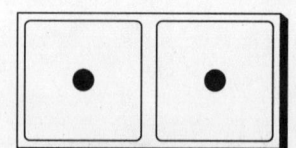

❶ 1 + 1 = ____

❷ 2 + 2 = ____

❸ 3 + 3 = ____

❹ 4 + 4 = ____

❺ 5 + 5 = ____

❻ 6 + 6 = ____

❼ 7 + 7 = ____

❽ 8 + 8 = ____

❾ 9 + 9 = ____

110   Module 6: Section A, Lesson 1   © Houghton Mifflin Company. All rights reserved/1

Name _____

Materials: Crayons

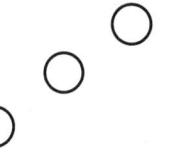

Draw to make doubles.
Complete the number sentences.

1) ○ ○ ○
○ ○ ○

6 + 6 = ____

2) ○   ○
○   ○

4 + 4 = ____

3)   ○
   ○
○

3 + ___ = ____

4) ○ ○ ○
○   ○
○ ○ ○

8 + ___ = ____

5) ○ ○ ○
   ○
○ ○ ○

7 + ___ = ____

6) ○   ○
   ○
○   ○

5 + ___ = ____

7) ○ ○ ○
○ ○ ○
○ ○ ○

9 + ___ = ____

8)   ○
   ○

2 + ___ = ____

© Houghton Mifflin Company. All rights reserved/1

Module 6: Section A, Lesson 2   111

Name _____

Draw the missing part.
Complete the number sentence.

1 10 in all

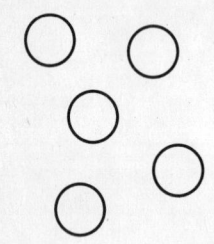

10 − 5 = ____

2 14 in all

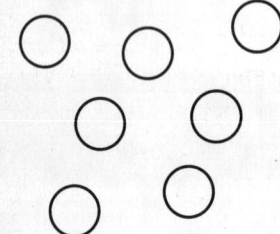

14 − ____ = ____

3 8 in all

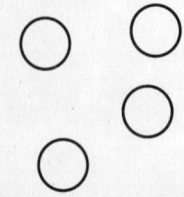

8 − ____ = ____

4 16 in all

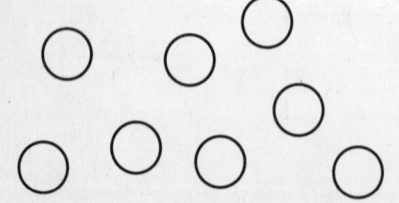

16 − ____ = ____

Name _____

The bees belong to fact families.
Match the bees to their hives.
Complete the fact families.

Hive 5: 5-2=___
Hive 7:
Hive 9:
Hive 8:

Bees: 5-2, 6+1, 9-4, 2+3, 7-1, 4+5, 4+4, 8-4

Module 6: Section A, Lesson 4   113

Name _____

SKILL PLUS 88 WORKSHEET

Draw a picture.
Write a number sentence.

1 8 people ride in a boat.
4 jump in the water.
How many people still ride in the boat?

_____ - _____ = _____

2 12 children ride a train.
6 get off.
How many children are on the train?

_____ - _____ = _____

3 Try one of your own.

_____

_____

_____

_____ - _____ = _____

Name _____

Materials: Crayons

Color dimes silver or gray.
Color pennies brown.
Ring the amount.

① penny, dime, penny, penny   5¢   14¢   15¢

② dime, penny, penny   9¢   13¢   19¢

③ penny, dime, penny   12¢   17¢   19¢

④ dime, dime   2¢   11¢   20¢

⑤ penny, penny, penny, penny, penny, penny, penny, penny   11¢   14¢   18¢

⑥ penny, dime, penny, penny, penny, penny, penny, penny, penny, penny   5¢   10¢   20¢

Skill Plus Worksheet 89

Module 6: Section B, Lesson 6

Name _____

Show **2** ways to make each price.
Draw the coins.

Use 1¢, 10¢, 5¢.

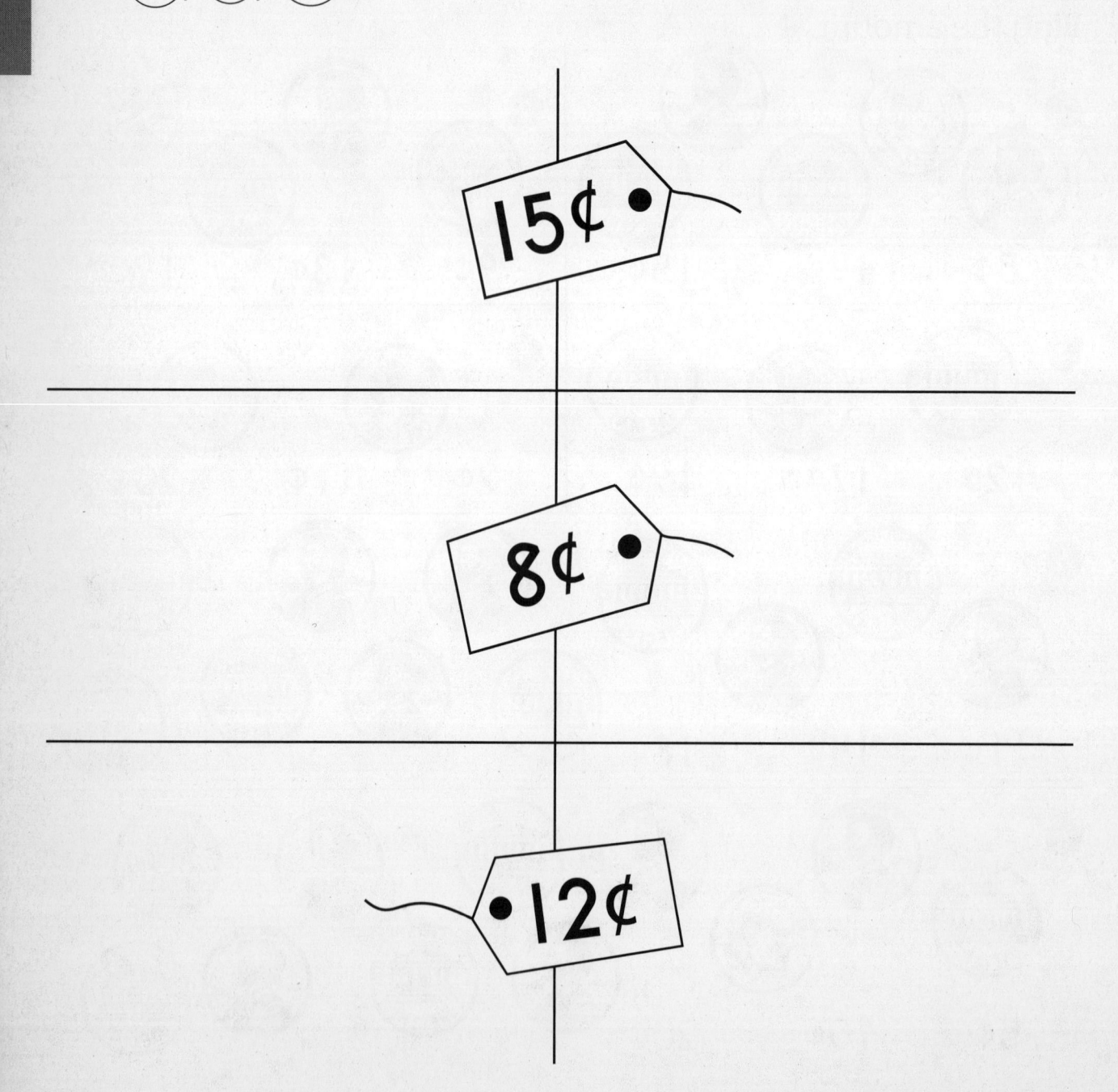

15¢

8¢

12¢

116   Module 6: Section B, Lesson 7

Name _____

Materials: Crayons

Is it a fair trade?
Color a face to show.

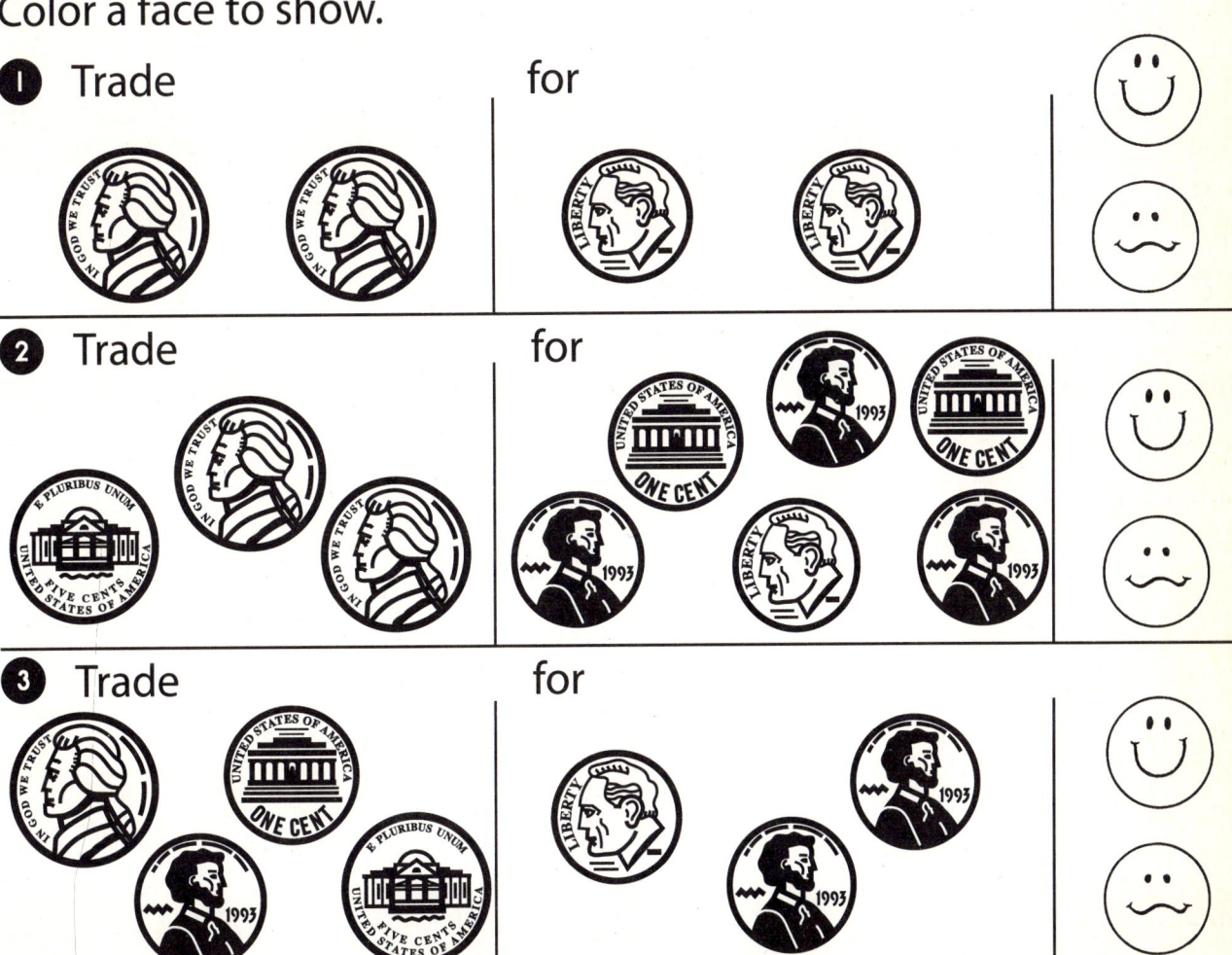

1 Trade   for

2 Trade   for

3 Trade   for

Show a fair trade.

4 Trade   for

Module 6: Section B, Lesson 7

Name _____

Materials: Coins

Find out how much money you have.
Act out the problems with coins.

	You Had	You Earned	You Spent	Now You Have
1	10¢	2¢	0¢	_____ ¢
2	8¢	0¢	5¢	_____ ¢
3	3¢	6¢	0¢	_____ ¢
4	2¢	5¢	5¢	_____ ¢
5	7¢	0¢	6¢	_____ ¢
6	5¢	1¢	2¢	_____ ¢
7	3¢	3¢	6¢	_____ ¢

Try some of your own.

	You Had	You Earned	You Spent	Now You Have
8	_____ ¢	_____ ¢	_____ ¢	_____ ¢
9	_____ ¢	_____ ¢	_____ ¢	_____ ¢

Module 6: Section B, Lesson 8 © Houghton Mifflin Company. All rights reserved/1

Name _____

There are 10 pennies.
How many pennies are in the bank?

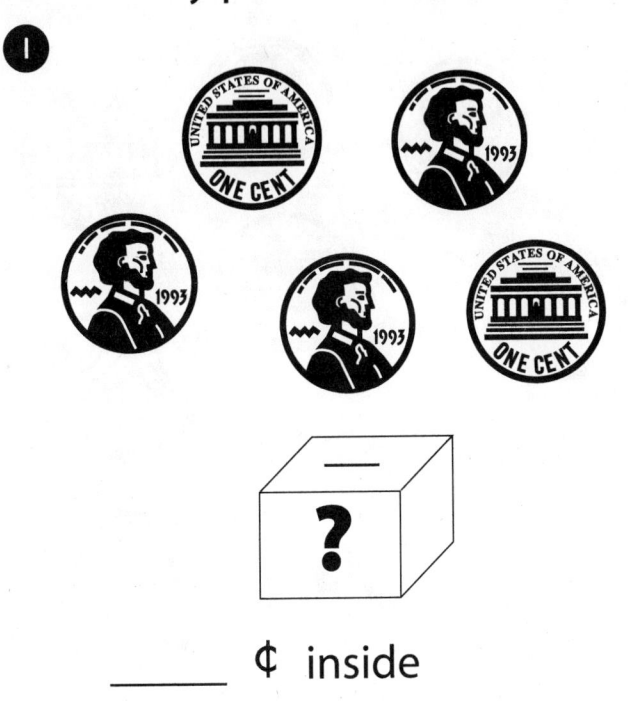

1.
____ ¢ inside

2.
____ ¢ inside

3.
____ ¢ inside

4.
____ ¢ inside

© Houghton Mifflin Company. All rights reserved/1   Module 6: Section B, Lesson 9

Name _____

Write the amounts.
Ring the greater amount.

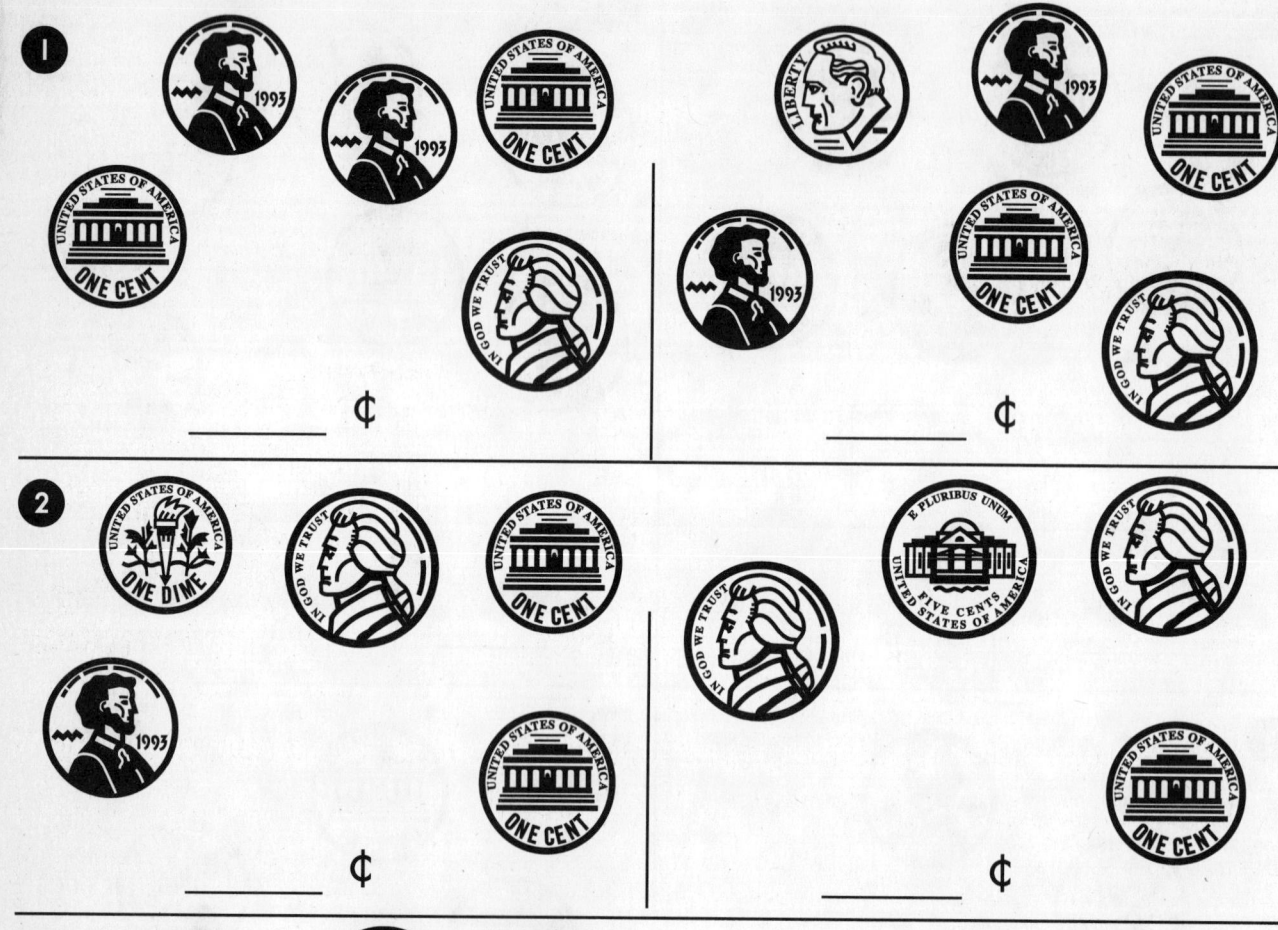

1. _____ ¢   _____ ¢

2. _____ ¢   _____ ¢

Draw a greater amount.

3. _____ ¢   _____ ¢

Name _____

Use the table.
Estimate the number.
Then tally and write the number.

Kind of Tool	Your Estimate	Tallies	Number in all
1			
2			
3			
4			

© Houghton Mifflin Company. All rights reserved/1

Module 6: Section C, Lesson 11

Name _____

Materials: Crayons

SKILL PLUS 96 WORKSHEET

Color the flowers in one group of ten.

Use the picture.

① Estimate the number of flowers.

about _____ flowers

② Ring groups of ten.

③ Count the flowers by tens.

Count on the ones.

_____ flowers in all

④ How did you estimate? _____
_____

⑤ How did coloring help? _____
_____

122 Module 6: Section C, Lesson 12   © Houghton Mifflin Company. All rights reserved/1

Name _____

Write a fact family for the picture.
Ring a fact.
Write a story about the fact.

1

2 + 8 = ____

____ + ____ = ____

10 − 2 = ____

____ − ____ = ____

_____

_____

_____

2

____ + ____ = ____

____ − ____ = ____

_____

_____

_____

© Houghton Mifflin Company. All rights reserved/1

Module 6: Section C, Lesson 13   123

Name _____

Materials: Crayons

Color ◯ green.

Color ⬭ yellow.

Count by threes.
Write the number of the yellow bead.

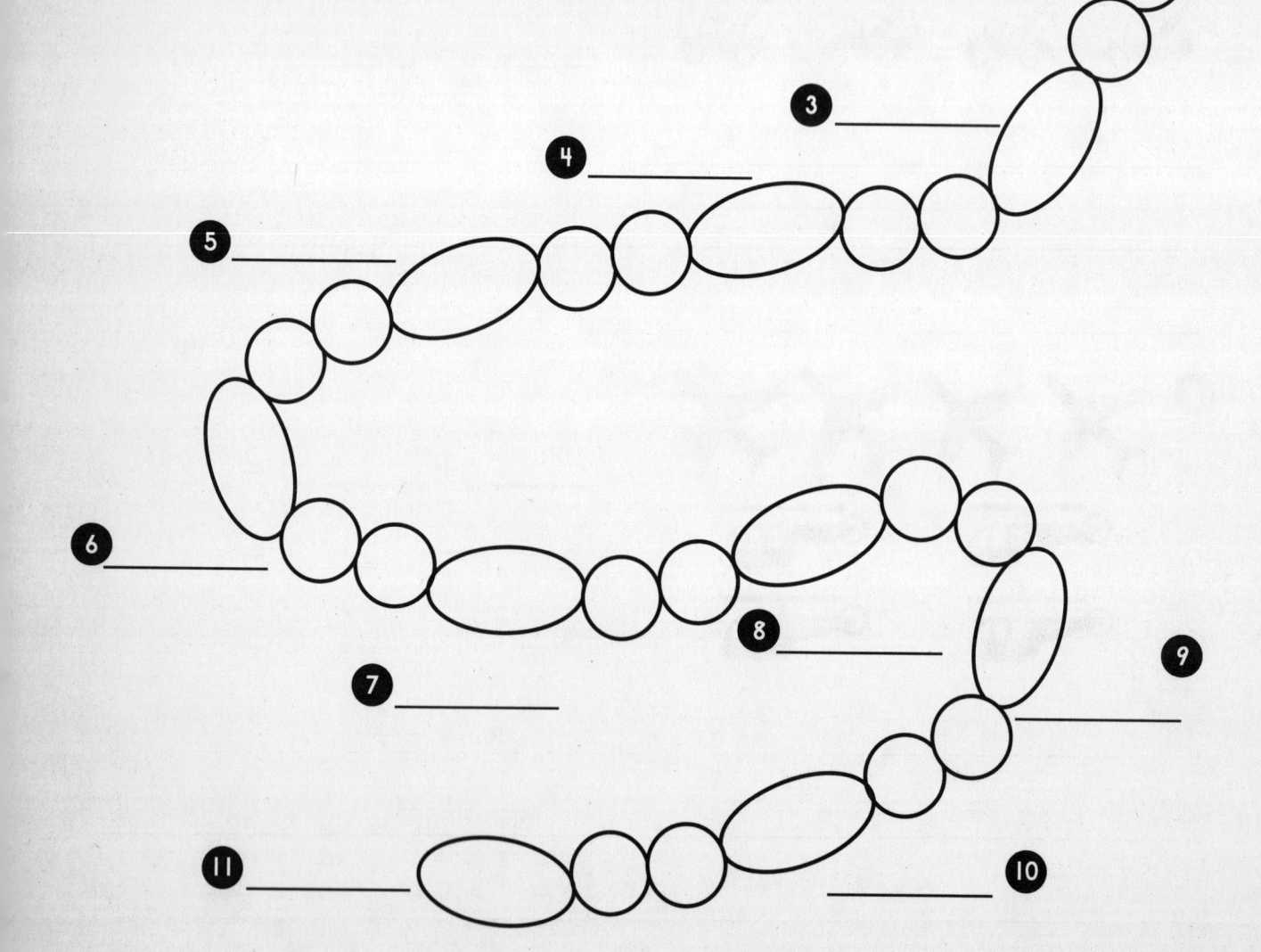

1. ___3___
2. _____
3. _____
4. _____
5. _____
6. _____
7. _____
8. _____
9. _____
10. _____
11. _____

124 Module 6: Section C, Lesson 14 © Houghton Mifflin Company. All rights reserved/1

Name _____

Materials: Crayons

Write the missing sums.

+	0	1	2	3	4	5	6
0	0	1		3	4	5	6
1	1	2	3	4	5	6	7
2	2		4	5	6		8
3	3	4	5		7	8	9
4	4	5	6	7	8	9	
5	5		7	8	9	10	
6		7	8	9	10	11	12

Add. Color your sums on the table.

1. 2 + 4 = _____ and 4 + 2 = _____ red

2. 5 + 0 = _____ and 0 + 5 = _____ orange

3. 6 + 5 = _____ and 5 + 6 = _____ yellow

4. 3 + 3 = _____ blue

Write about sums that are the same color.

5. _____

Name _____

Draw shapes. Write the numbers.

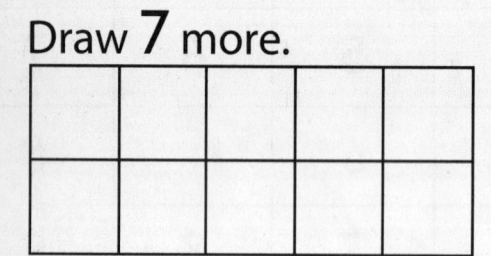

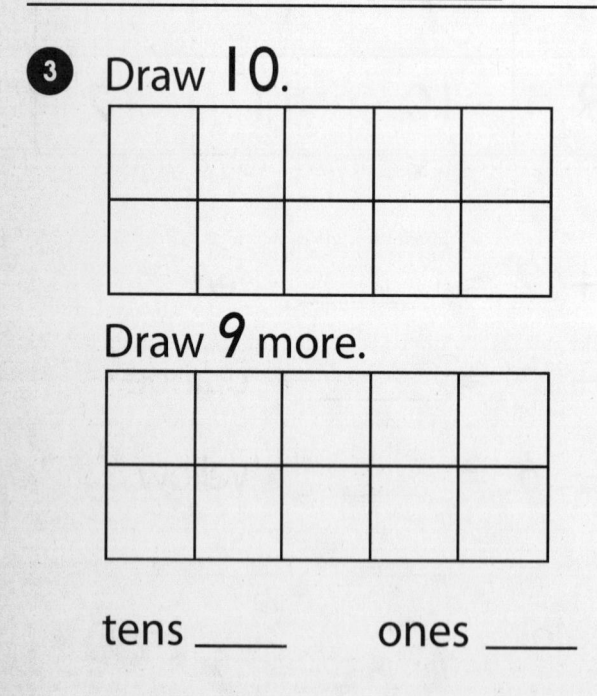

1 Draw 10.

Draw 7 more.

tens ____   ones ____

number in all _____

2 Draw 10.

Draw 3 more.

tens ____   ones ____

number in all _____

3 Draw 10.

Draw 9 more.

tens ____   ones ____

number in all _____

4 Draw 10.

Draw 6 more.

tens ____   ones ____

number in all _____

126   Module 7: Section A, Lesson 1

Name _____

SKILL PLUS 101 WORKSHEET

Materials: Your sticks or stones or other counters, place-value work mat 1

Show the number with objects.
Fill in the table.

	Show.	Draw what you show.	Write the numbers.	
			Tens	Ones
1	15			
2	17			
3	20			
4	14			

© Houghton Mifflin Company. All rights reserved/1

Module 7: Section A, Lesson 2   127

Name _____

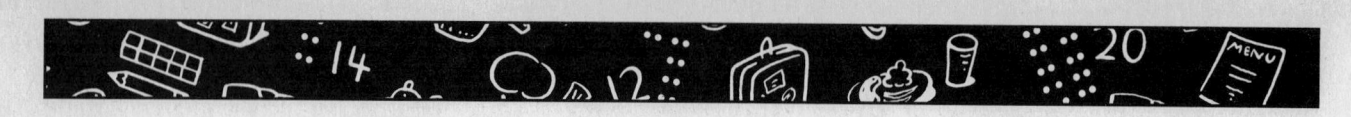

**Write the tens and ones.
Write the total.**

1.

Tens	Ones

_____

2.

Tens	Ones

_____

3.

Tens	Ones

_____

4.

Tens	Ones

_____

5.

Tens	Ones

_____

Name _____

Materials: Crayons

Match the numbers to the pictures.
Color.

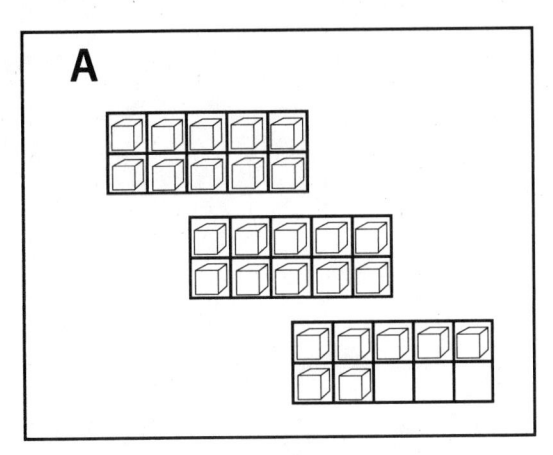

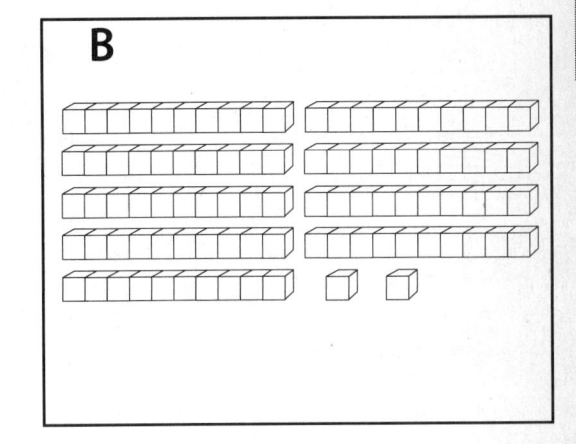

1. 58

2. 36

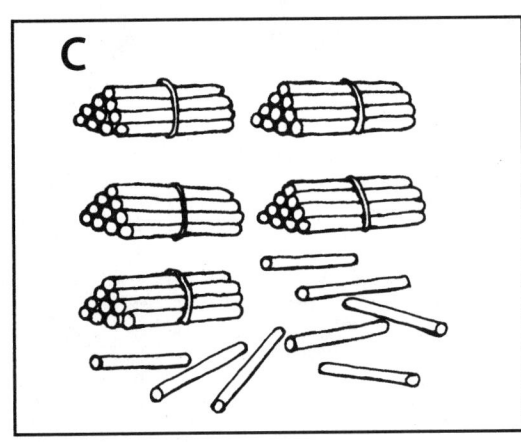

3. 92

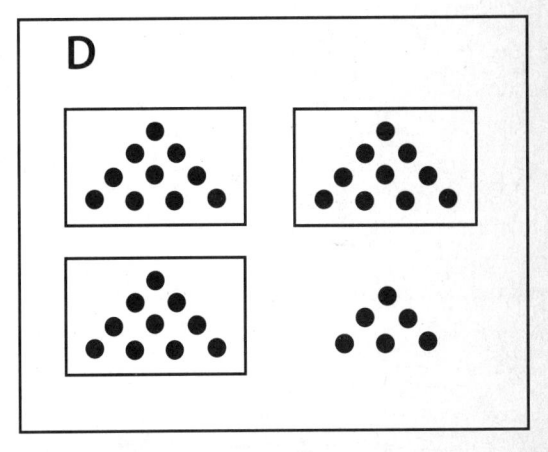

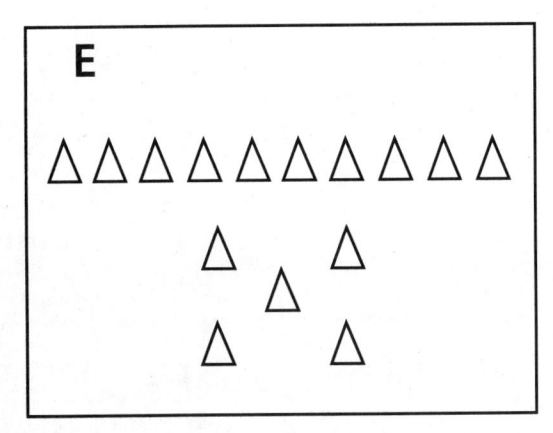

4. 70

5. 15

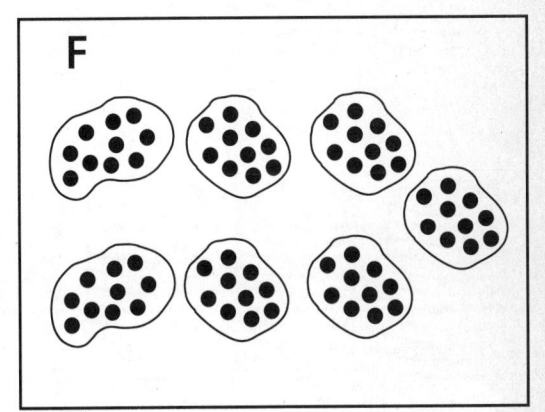

6. 27

Name _____

Materials: Dimes and pennies

Make piles like the picture.
Trade pennies for a dime when you can.
Write the numbers.

1. _____ dimes _____ pennies

2. _____ dimes _____ pennies

3. _____ dimes _____ pennies

4. _____ dimes _____ pennies

130 Module 7: Section A, Lesson 5

Name _____

Materials: Pennies and dimes

Choose coins to pay for the food.
Draw the coins.

1

VEGETABLE
Peas

29¢ a bowl

2

SOUP
Miso Soup

35¢ a bowl

3

SALAD
Green Salad

42¢ a bowl

Name _____

Write the amounts.
Ring the greater amount.

1. _____ ¢   _____ ¢

2. _____ ¢   _____ ¢

3. _____ ¢   _____ ¢

4. _____ ¢   _____ ¢

132   Module 7: Section B, Lesson 7   © Houghton Mifflin Company. All rights reserved/1

Name _____

Materials: Pennies, nickels, dimes, quarters

Lay coins on top of their pictures.

Sort the coins into **2** groups.
Draw the groups in the boxes.

How did you sort? _____

_____

Name _____

Materials: Brown and yellow crayons

Find the number. Color its box brown.

1. 1 less than 48
2. 1 more than 13
3. 10 + 5
4. 10 more than 7
5. 10 less than 36
6. 10 less than 47
7. 4 tens and 6 ones
8. 20 + 4
9. 10 + 10 + 10 + 10 + 4
10. 4 tens and 5 ones
11. 10 more than 17
12. 1 more than 15
13. 37 − 1
14. 10 + 10 + 10 + 4
15. 10 less than 35
16. 30 + 5
17. 4 tens and 3 ones
18. 1 less than 49

Color the other boxes yellow.

1	2	3	4	5	6	7	8	9	10
11	12	13	14	15	16	17	18	19	20
21	22	23	24	25	26	27	28	29	30
31	32	33	34	35	36	37	38	39	40
41	42	43	44	45	46	47	48	49	50
51	52	53	54	55	56	57	58	59	60

What picture did you make? _____

Name _____

Materials: Pennies and dimes

Place coins in the boxes.
Write the cost of both items.

Dimes	Pennies

1. 18¢ 6¢ _____ ¢

2. 25¢ 12¢ _____ ¢

3. 39¢ 16¢ _____ ¢

© Houghton Mifflin Company. All rights reserved/1   Module 7: Section B, Lesson 9

Name _____

The amount changes.
Ring what happens.
Write the number.

SKILL PLUS 110 WORKSHEET

1. from 5¢ to 7¢   subtract ____¢   add ____¢
2. from 9¢ to 6¢   subtract ____¢   add ____¢
3. from 11¢ to 9¢   subtract ____¢   add ____¢
4. from 4¢ to 8¢   subtract ____¢   add ____¢
5. from 3¢ to 6¢   subtract ____¢   add ____¢
6. from 8¢ to 5¢   subtract ____¢   add ____¢
7. from 10¢ to 4¢   subtract ____¢   add ____¢
8. from 6¢ to 2¢   subtract ____¢   add ____¢
9. from 1¢ to 7¢   subtract ____¢   add ____¢

Make up your own.

10. from ____¢
    to   ____¢   subtract ____¢   add ____¢

136   Module 7: Section B, Lesson 10   © Houghton Mifflin Company. All rights reserved/1

Name _____

Materials: Centimeter rods and cubes

Estimate the length.
Then measure.

1

Estimate. _____ centimeters   Measure. _____ centimeters

2

Estimate. _____ centimeters   Measure. _____ centimeters

3

Estimate. _____ centimeters   Measure. _____ centimeters

4

Estimate. _____ centimeters   Measure. _____ centimeters

© Houghton Mifflin Company. All rights reserved/1   Module 7: Section C, Lesson 11

Name _____

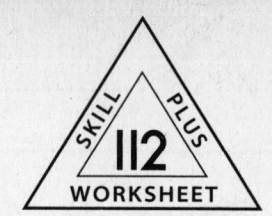

Materials: Centimeter ruler

Estimate.

① Which distance is the longest?

from letter _____ to letter _____

② Which distance is the shortest?

from letter _____ to letter _____

Measure.

③ from A to B about _____ centimeters

④ from A to D about _____ centimeters

⑤ from B to C about _____ centimeters

⑥ from B to D about _____ centimeters

⑦ from C to D about _____ centimeters

⑧ from A to C about _____ centimeters

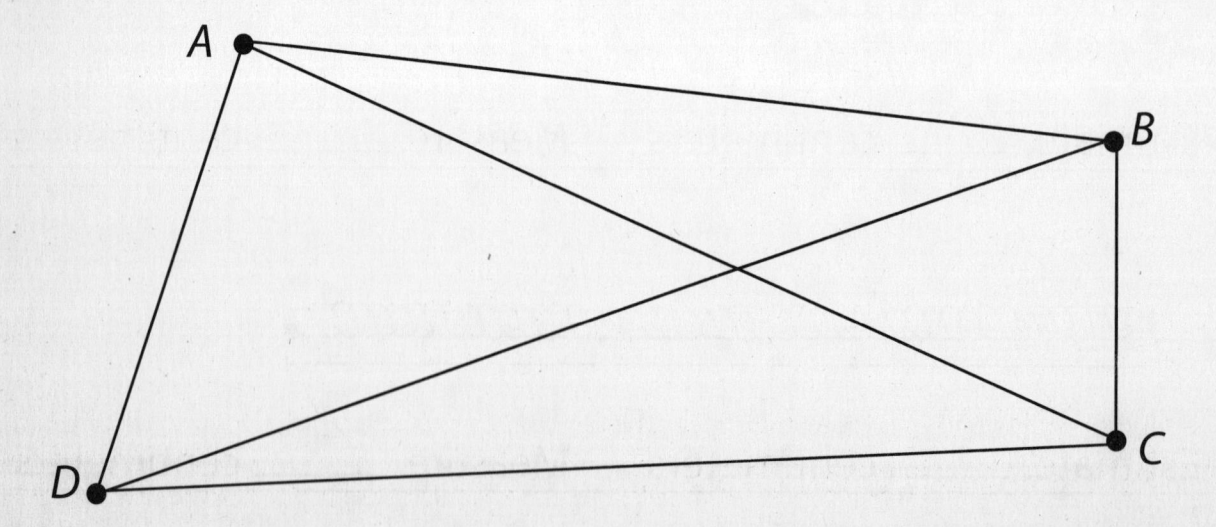

138 Module 7: Section C, Lesson 11

Name _____

Materials: Crayons, centimeter ruler

Read the table.
Plan a drawing.
Then draw.

Object	Measurement
person	12 centimeters
tree	14 centimeters
pet	5 centimeters
park bench	10 centimeters

Draw another object in your picture.
What is its measurement? _____

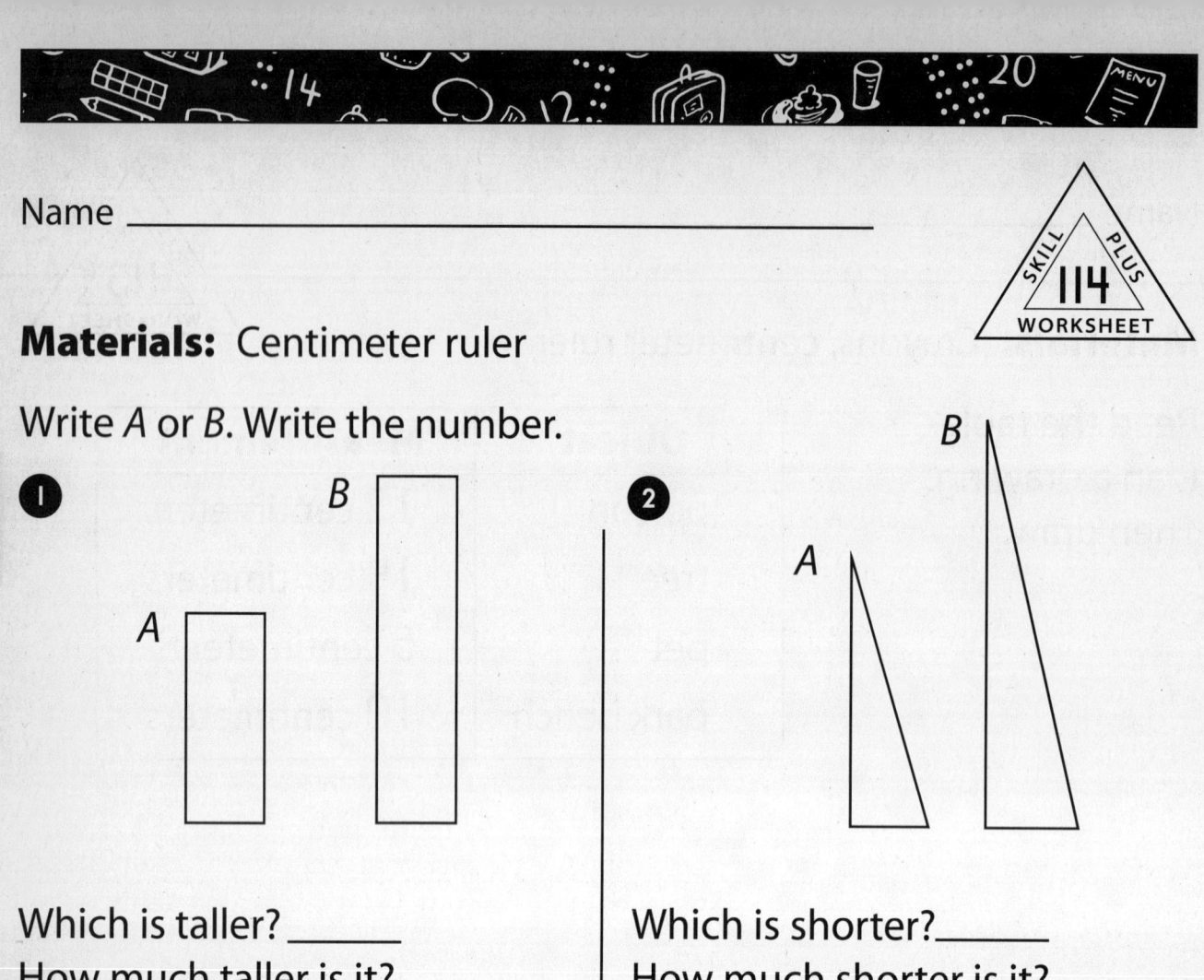

Name _____

Materials: Centimeter ruler

Write A or B. Write the number.

1

Which is taller? _____
How much taller is it?

_____ centimeters

2

Which is shorter? _____
How much shorter is it?

_____ centimeters

3

Which is shorter? _____
How much shorter is it?

_____ centimeters

4 A   B

Draw.
Make A taller than B.
How much taller is A?

_____ centimeters

140   Module 7: Section C, Lesson 13   © Houghton Mifflin Company. All rights reserved/1

Name _____

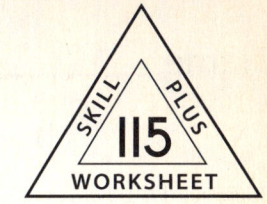

Materials: Crayons, centimeter ruler

Look around you.
Draw pictures or write to show what you find.

❶ objects shorter than 15 centimeters	❷ objects longer than 15 centimeters

Draw an animal.

❸ shorter than 15 centimeters

❹ longer than 15 centimeters

Name _____

SKILL PLUS 116 WORKSHEET

Which shape is hiding?
Read the clues.
Ring the shape.
Write its name.

Shapes
circle   rectangle
square   triangle

1

clues
3 sides
3 corners

2

clues
no corners
1 curved side

3

clues
4 sides
4 corners
2 longer sides
2 shorter sides

4

clues
4 sides
4 corners
All sides are the same length.

Name _____

Materials: Geoboard, rubber bands

Make the shapes on a geoboard.
Draw what you make.

1 1 large square and
1 small square

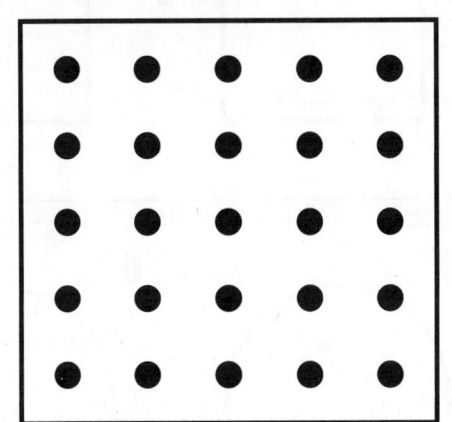

2 a shape with 5 sides

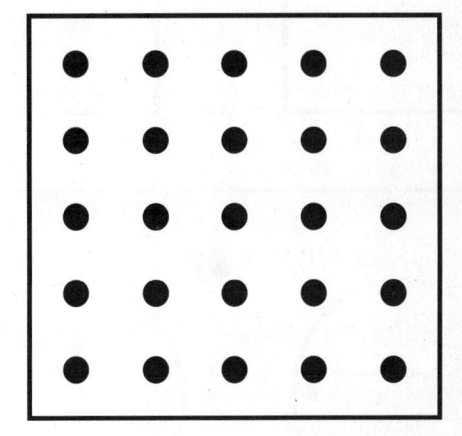

3 3 triangles of different sizes

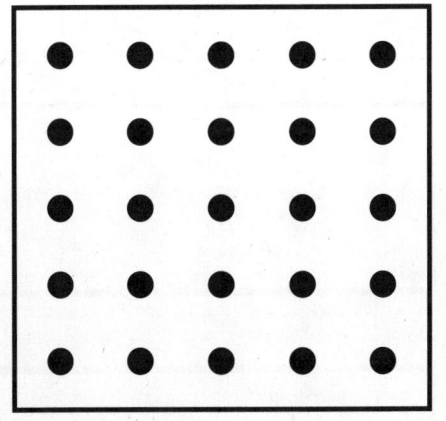

4 a shape like this

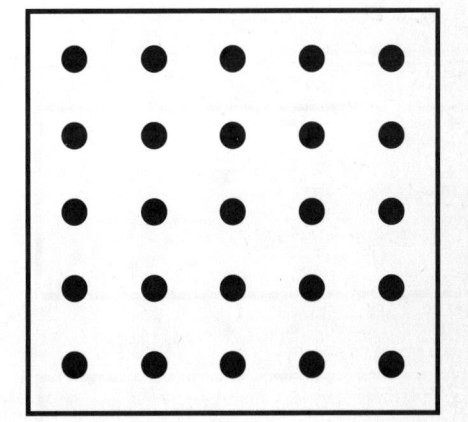

Write about them. _____

Write about it. _____

_____

_____

© Houghton Mifflin Company. All rights reserved/1

Module 8: Section A, Lesson 2   143

Name _____

Materials: Red and blue crayons

Draw different ways to make halves.
Color one half red and one half blue.

1.
2.
3.
4.

5.
6.
7.
8.

9.
10.
11.
12.

144   Module 8: Section A, Lesson 3   © Houghton Mifflin Company. All rights reserved/1

Name _____

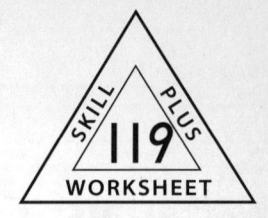

Materials: Crayons

Color the quilt patches.
Use yellow and green for halves.
Use orange and brown for fourths.

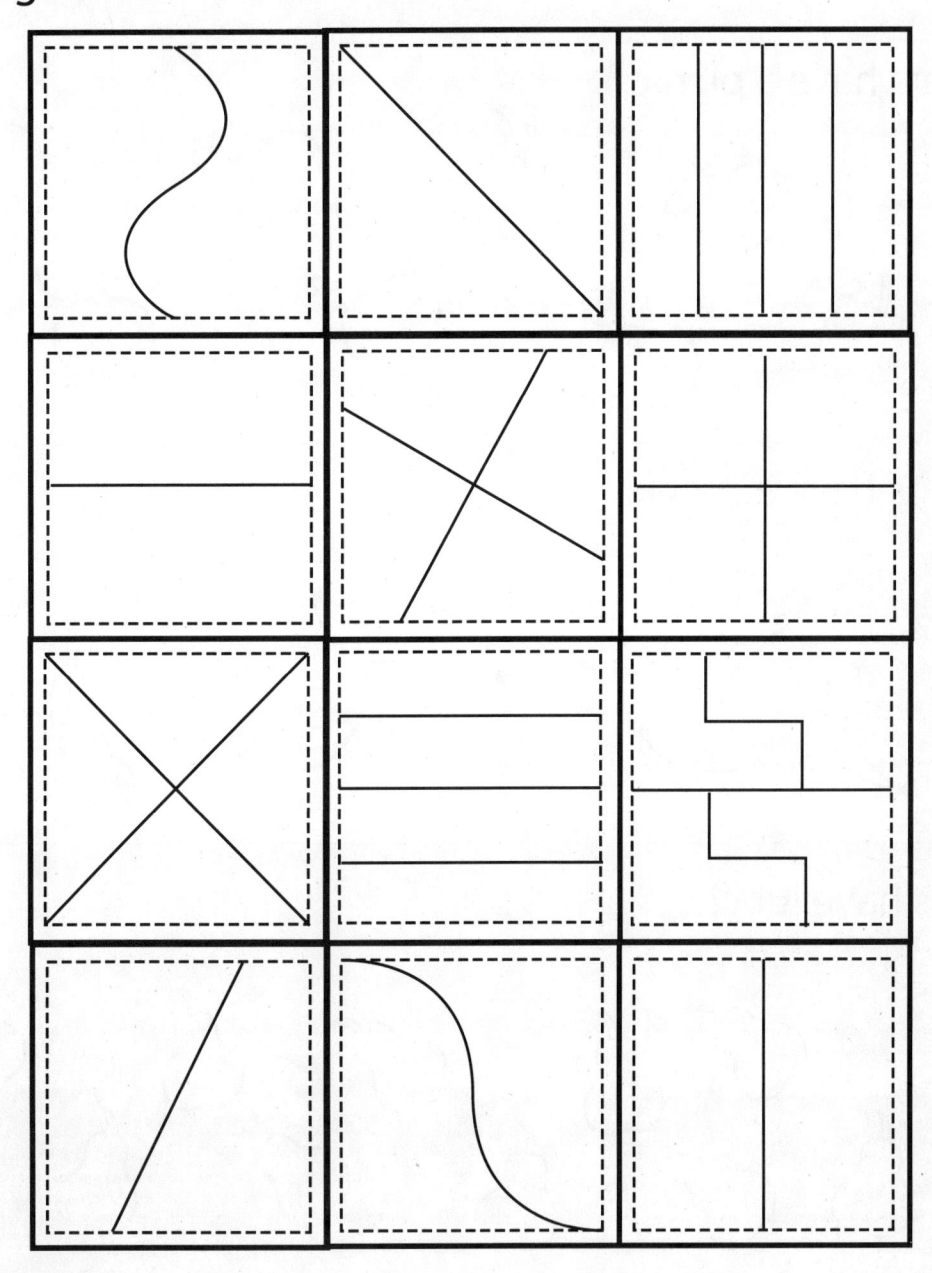

Module 8: Section A, Lesson 4 145

Name _____

Materials: Crayons

Show how the animals can share.
Ring equal parts.
Color.

① **3** bears have a picnic.

② **4** goats have a snack.

③ **3** pigs have lunch.

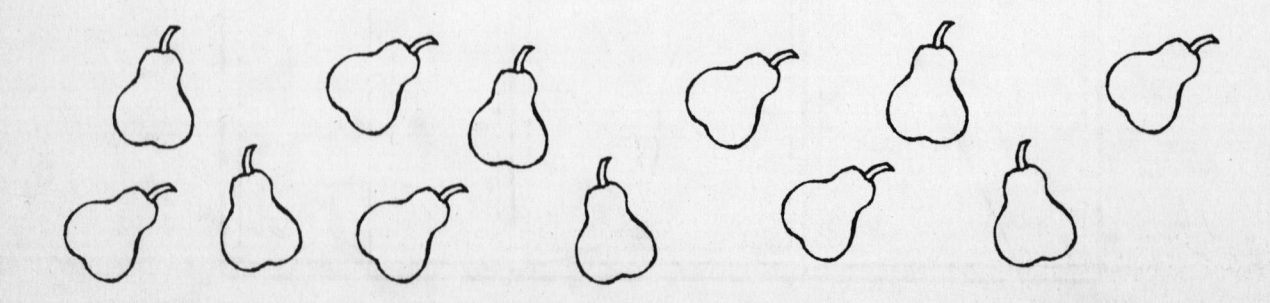

146 Module 8: Section A, Lesson 5

Name _____

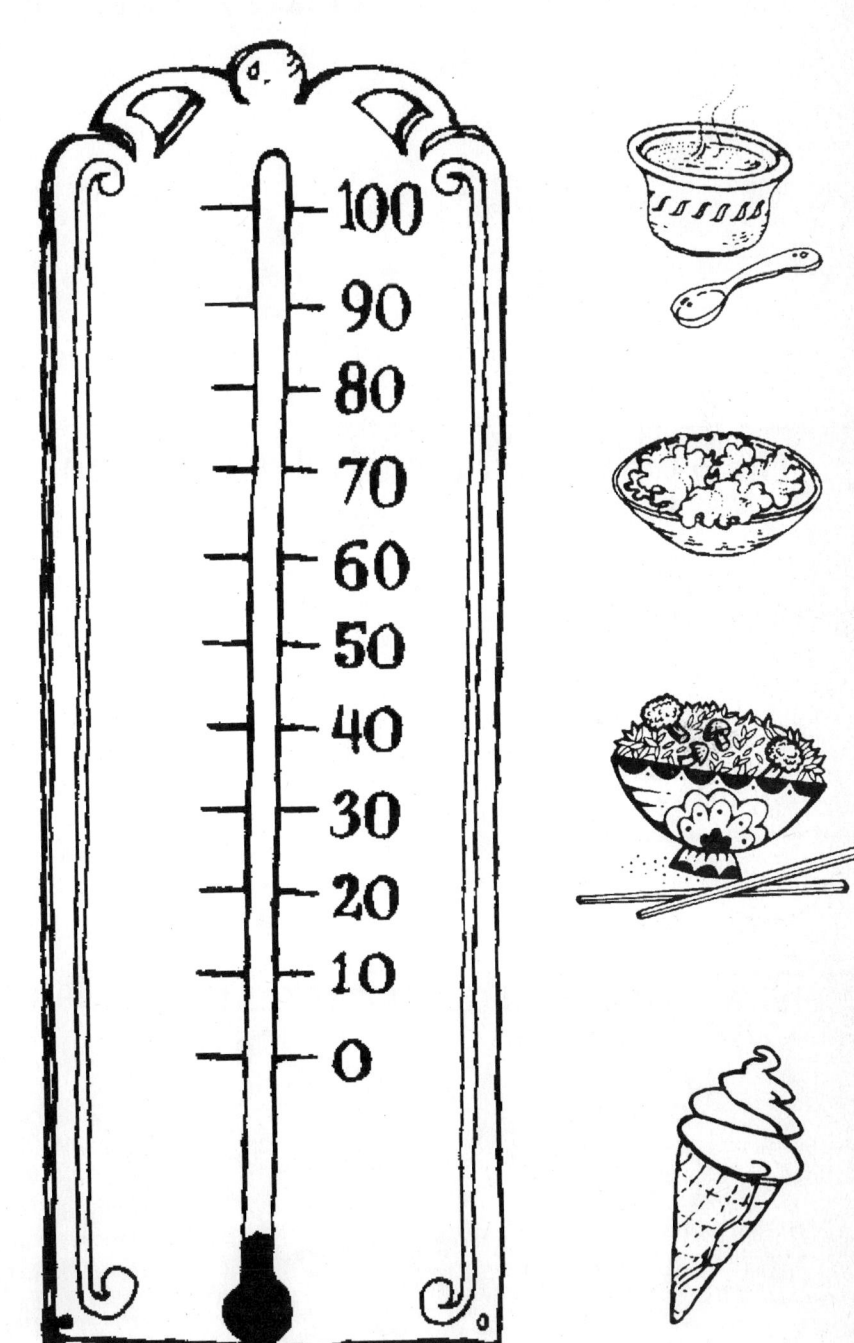

SKILL PLUS 121 WORKSHEET

Match the temperature to the thermometer.
Match the thermometer to the object.

1 30 degrees

2 50 degrees

3 80 degrees

4 100 degrees

© Houghton Mifflin Company. All rights reserved/1

Module 8: Section B, Lesson 6   147

Name _____

Materials: Crayons

1 Draw what you do that takes about a minute.

2 Draw what you do that takes less than a minute.

3 Draw what you do that takes more than a minute.

Name _____

Materials: Crayons

Write the time.
What might you be doing then?
Draw or write.

1 ___:___

2 ___:___

3 ___:___

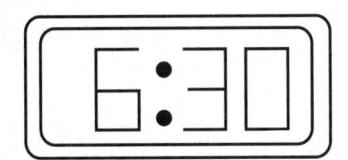

4 ___:___

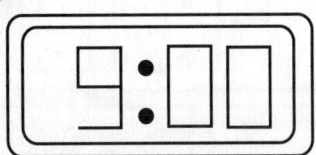

© Houghton Mifflin Company. All rights reserved/1

Module 8: Section B, Lesson 8   149

Name _____

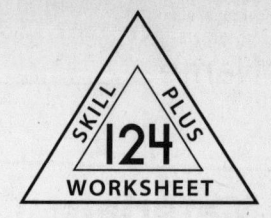

SKILL PLUS 124 WORKSHEET

Draw and write the missing time.

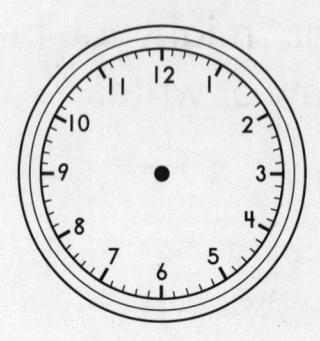

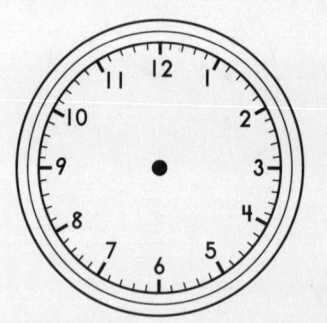

Start	Time It Takes	Finish
1 Drive to a friend's house. 9:00	**2** hours	(clock face) ___:___
2 Start cooking dinner. 5:30	**30** minutes	(clock face) ___:___
3 Go to the zoo. (clock face)	**3** hours	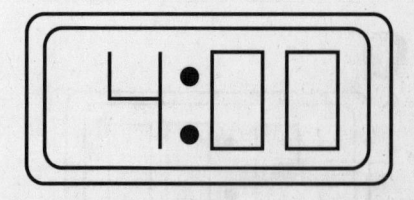 4:00 4:00

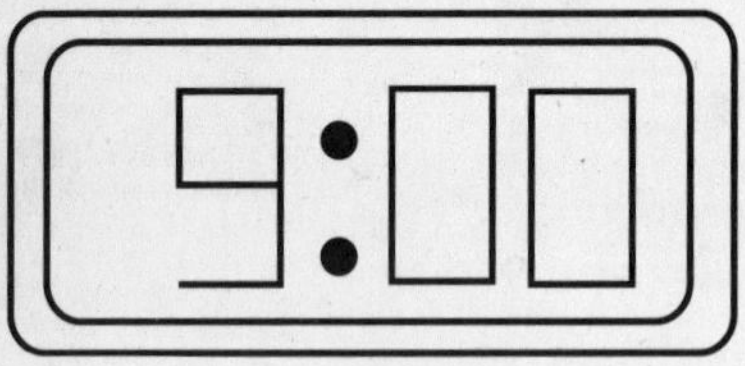

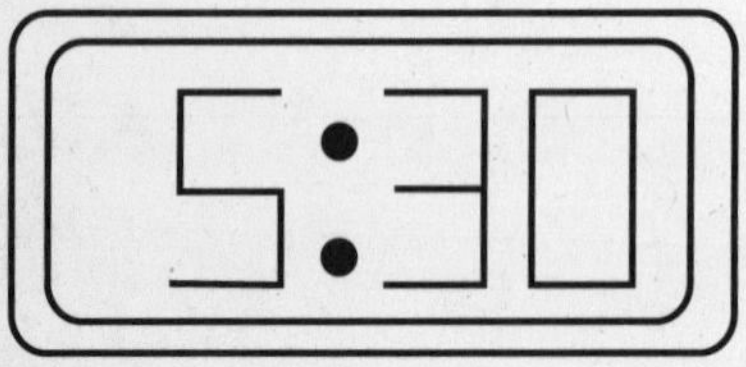

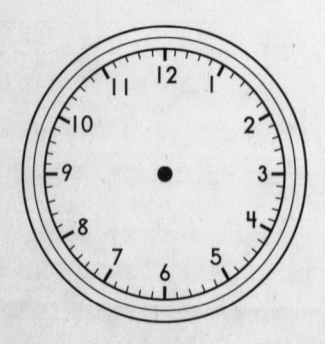

150   Module 8: Section B, Lesson 9 © Houghton Mifflin Company. All rights reserved/1

Name _____

Materials: Crayons

What might you do on Saturday?
Show the time.

1 Get up.

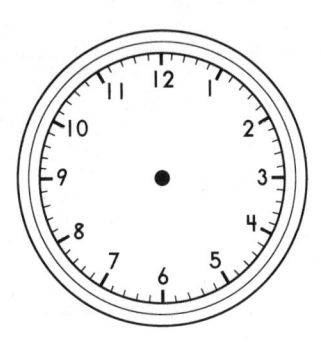

____ : ____

2 Eat Lunch.

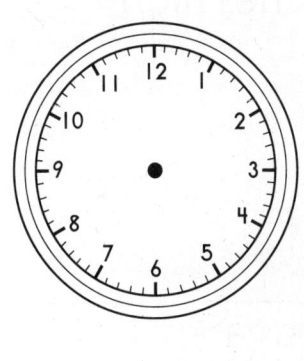

____ : ____

3 Go to _____.

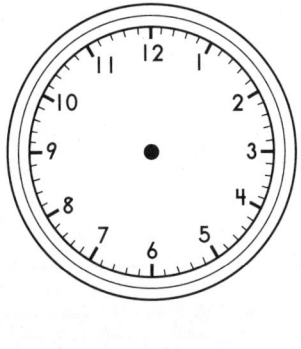

____ : ____

4 Talk to _____.

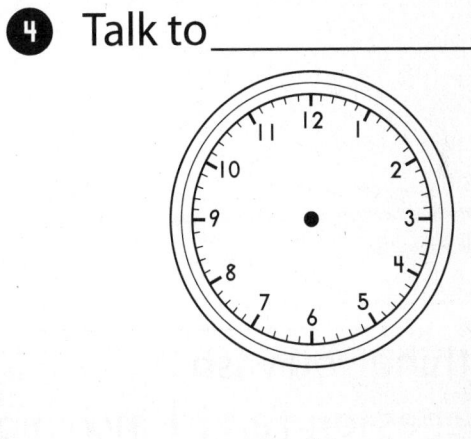

____ : ____

5 What is your favorite time on Saturday? Why? _____
_____
_____

Name _____

Materials: Crayons, inch ruler

Draw.

1. a ticket to a show
   3 inches long,
   2 inches high

2. bookmark
   6 inches long, 1 inch high

3. anything you wish
   5 inches long and 1 inch high

What did you draw? _____

Name _____

Materials: Crayons

Draw the objects on the scales.
Ring the heavier one.

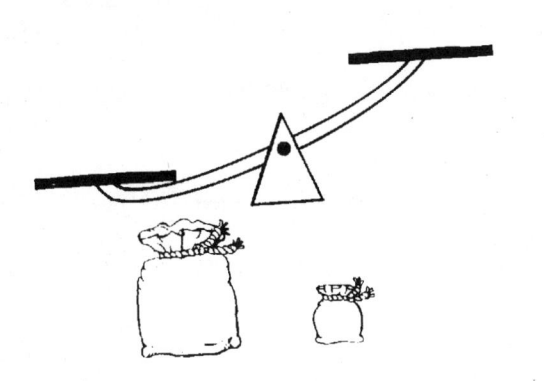

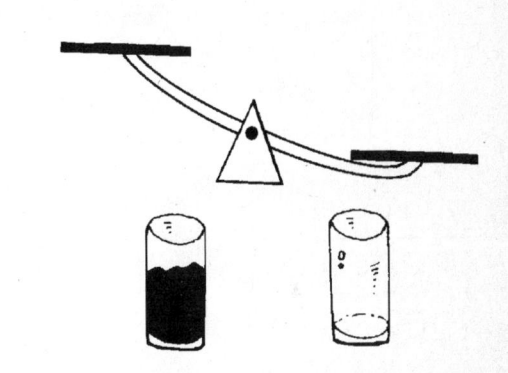

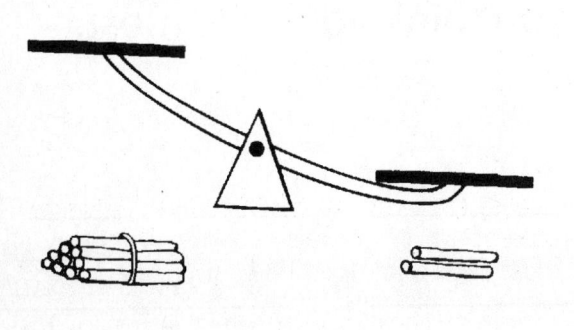

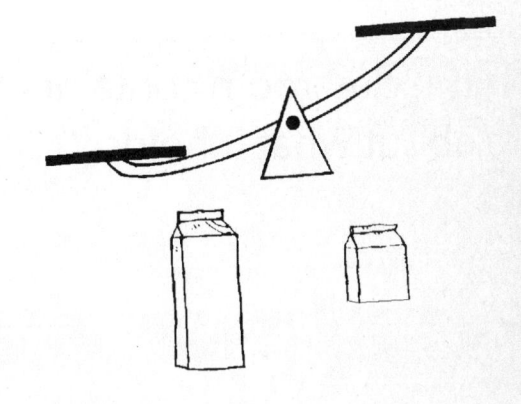

❶

❷

❸

❹

© Houghton Mifflin Company. All rights reserved/1

Module 8: Section C, Lesson 11   153

Name _____

Materials: Crayons

Ring the container that holds the least.
Color.

1.

2.

Ring the container that hold the most.
Color.

3.

4.

Draw the classroom container that you think holds the most.
Write about what it holds.

5.

_____

_____

_____

154   Module 8: Section C, Lesson 12

Name _____

About how many □ will fit?
Write an estimate.
Then draw squares and count.

Estimate.   **Count.**

1

2

3

4

© Houghton Mifflin Company. All rights reserved/1   Module 8: Section C, Lesson 13   155

Name _____

Write the additions in their boxes.
Add.

7 + 7	5 + 1	9 + 9	1 + 7
0 + 8	4 + 6	3 + 1	6 + 0
2 + 8	8 + 8	7 + 3	6 + 1
6 + 6	0 + 9	8 + 2	6 + 4

Adding 0

___ + ___ = ___

___ + ___ = ___

___ + ___ = ___

Counting On 1

___ + ___ = ___

___ + ___ = ___

___ + ___ = ___

___ + ___ = ___

Doubles

___ + ___ = ___

___ + ___ = ___

___ + ___ = ___

___ + ___ = ___

Making 10

___ + ___ = ___

___ + ___ = ___

___ + ___ = ___

___ + ___ = ___

Module 9: Section A, Lesson 1

Name _____

Match the doubles to their doubles plus one facts. Add.

❶
```
  8
+ 9
___
```

6 + 7 = ____

5 + 4 = ____

6 + 6 = ____

4 + 4 = ____

```
  8
+ 8
___
```

```
  1
+ 2
___
```

1 + 1 = ____

7 + 7 = ____

```
  7
+ 8
___
```

Which double helps you to add?
Ring the double.
Then add.

❷ 8 + 7 = ____   5 + 5   7 + 7

❸ 9 + 8 = ____   8 + 8   6 + 3

❹ 7 + 6 = ____   6 + 6   6 + 4

Name _____

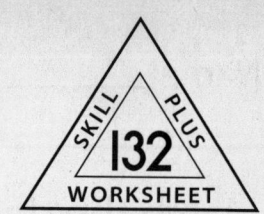

Materials: Red and blue crayons

Use the ten-frame.
Draw the numbers of dots.
Write the number sentence.

1 8 red dots   6 blue dots

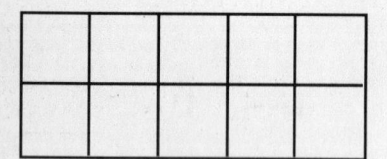

_____ + _____ = _____

2 6 red dots   5 blue dots

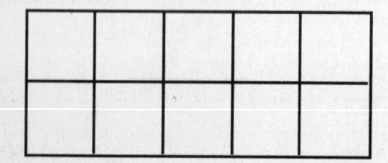

_____ + _____ = _____

3 7 red dots   7 blue dots

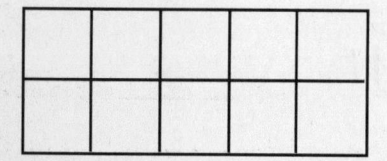

_____ + _____ = _____

4 9 red dots   4 blue dots

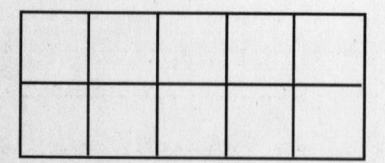

_____ + _____ = _____

5 _____ red dots   _____ blue dots

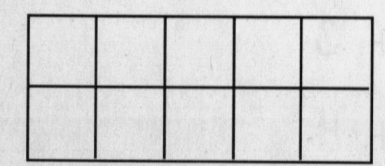

_____ + _____ = _____

158 Module 9: Section A, Lesson 3

Name _____

SKILL PLUS WORKSHEET 133

Materials: Crayons

Which number sentence has the same parts and whole? Color its picture frame to match.
Add and subtract.

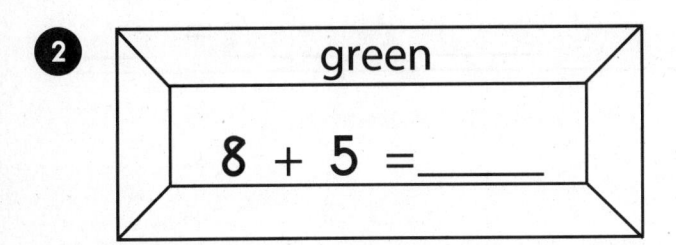

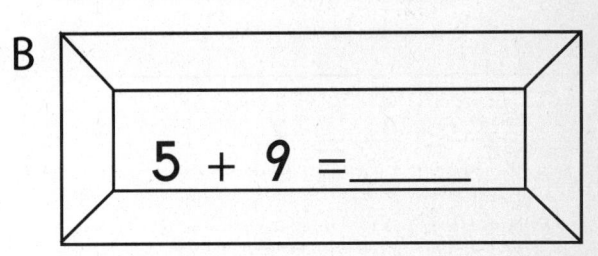

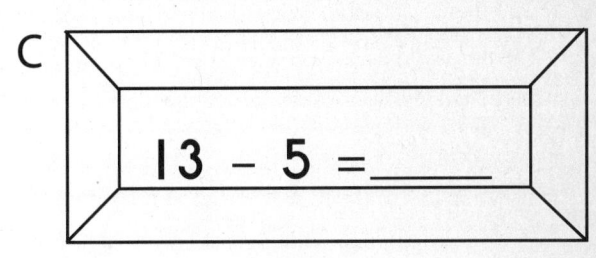

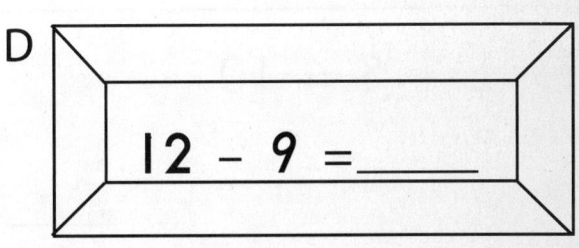

1. yellow
   14 − 5 = ____

2. green
   8 + 5 = ____

3. brown
   9 + 3 = ____

4. orange
   10 − 1 = ____

5. blue
   6 + 7 = ____

A. 13 − 7 = ____

B. 5 + 9 = ____

C. 13 − 5 = ____

D. 12 − 9 = ____

E. 1 + 9 = ____

© Houghton Mifflin Company. All rights reserved/1

Module 9: Section A, Lesson 4   159

Name _____

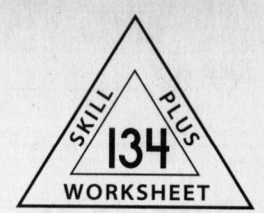

Draw a picture story about the fact.
Then complete the fact family.

1 5 + 4 = 9

4 + 5 = ____

9 – 5 = ____

____ – ____ = ____

2 7 – 1 = 6

____ + ____ = ____

____ + ____ = ____

____ – ____ = ____

3 2 + 8 = 10

____ + ____ = ____

____ – ____ = ____

____ – ____ = ____

160 Module 9: Section A, Lesson 5 © Houghton Mifflin Company. All rights reserved/1

Name _____

Materials: Base-ten materials

Show the numbers with tens and ones.
Ring the greater number.

Tens	Ones

❶	18	42	❷	23	31
❸	47	58	❹	53	35
❺	73	49	❻	21	12
❼	17	27	❽	33	13
❾	19	90	❿	24	29

© Houghton Mifflin Company. All rights reserved/1

Module 9: Section B, Lesson 6

Name _____

Add.

1) 14 + 10 = _____   2) 22 + 10 = _____

3) 75 + 10 = _____   4) 57 + 10 = _____

5) 83 + 10 = _____   6) 40 + 10 = _____

7) 51 + 10 = _____   8) 39 + 10 = _____

What happens to a number when you add 10?

9) _____
_____

Use what you know about 10 to add.

10) 52 + 20 = _____   11) 18 + 30 = _____

12) 47 + 40 = _____   13) 29 + 20 = _____

How did you find the answers?

14) _____
_____
_____

Write the missing numbers.

15) 17 + _____ = 20   16) 51 + _____ = 60

17) 29 + _____ = 30   18) 45 + _____ = 50

19) 63 + _____ = 70   20) 32 + _____ = 40

Module 9: Section B, Lesson 7 © Houghton Mifflin Company. All rights reserved/1

Name _____

Use the number line to help you solve.

0 5 10 15 20 25 30 35

1. I am **7** years old. How old will I be in **12** years?

_____ years old

2. How old am I now? **5** years ago I was **15**.

_____ years old

3. I am **19** years old. How old was I **6** years ago?

_____ years old

4. Add **3** to my age and you get **12**. How old am I?

_____ years old

5. How old will I be in **11** years? I am **8** years old now.

_____ years old

6. I am **3** years older than my sister. My sister is **12**. How old am I?

_____ years old

Write your own.

7. _____

_____

_____

© Houghton Mifflin Company. All rights reserved/1   Module 9: Section B, Lesson 8   163

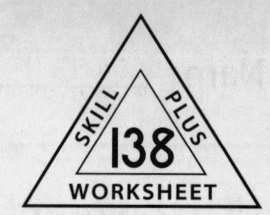

Name _____

Estimate.
Ring the closest answer.

1. 14 + 7   20   30   40
2. 28 + 3   20   30   40
3. 22 + 8   10   20   30
4. 19 + 12   21   31   41
5. 15 + 10   16   25   34
6. 35 + 11   35   45   55
7. 38 + 7   25   35   45
8. 17 + 14   20   30   40
9. 21 + 8   20   30   40
10. 32 + 19   40   50   60

Write about your work.

11. Which estimate seemed easy? Why? _____

12. Which estimate seemed hard? Why? _____

Name _____

Materials: Dimes and pennies

Use coins to help you solve.

Dimes	**Pennies**

	old price	Price Changes went up	Price Changes went down	new price
1	18¢	5¢		____ ¢
2	29¢		2¢	____ ¢
3	37¢	6¢		____ ¢
4	49¢	11¢		____ ¢
5	55¢		____ ¢	50¢

© Houghton Mifflin Company. All rights reserved/1

Module 9: Section B, Lesson 10   165

Name _____

Materials: Crayons

Draw the food in the groups.
Complete the sentence.

1 3 groups of 4 apples

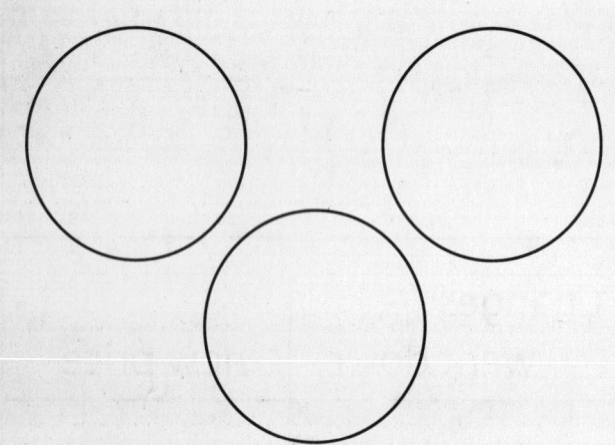

3 groups of 4 is _____.

2 4 groups of 4 pears

4 groups of 4 is _____.

3 5 groups of 3 peas

5 groups of 3 is _____.

4 5 groups of 2 nuts

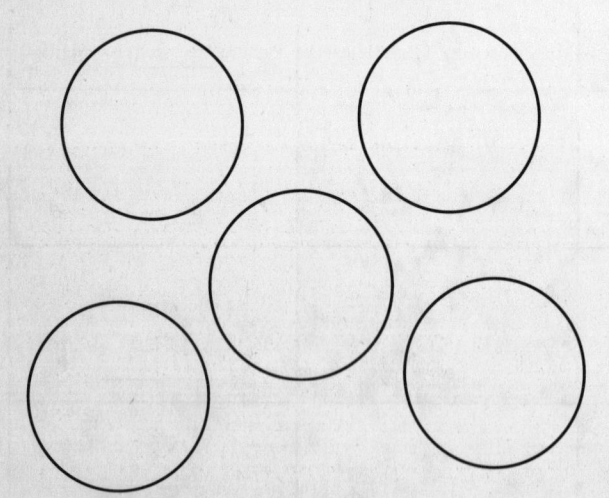

5 groups of 2 is _____.

166   Module 9: Section C, Lesson 11

Name _____

Materials: Calculator

Press the keys shown.
Write what you see in the display.

1. 6 [+] 4 [=] ___ [=] ___ [=] ___ [=] ___ [=] ___

Write about the number pattern. _____

_____

2. 20 [−] 2 [=] ___ [=] ___ [=] ___ [=] ___ [=] ___

Write about the number pattern. _____

_____

3. 11 [+] 3 [=] ___ [=] ___ [=] ___ [=] ___ [=] ___

Write about the number pattern. _____

_____

4. 19 [−] 3 [=] ___ [+] 3 [=] ___ [−] 3 [=] ___ [+] 3 [=] ___

Write about the number pattern. _____

_____

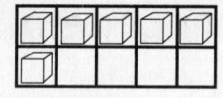

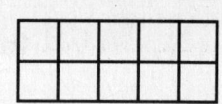

Name _____

**Draw to continue the patterns.
Write the numbers.**

1.

____ ____ ____ ____ ____

2.

____ ____ ____ ____ ____

3.

____ ____ ____ ____ ____

4.

____ ____ ____ ____ ____

168   Module 9: Section C, Lesson 13

Name _____

Materials: Crayons

How many different yogurt
treats can you make?
Use 1 flavor and 1 holder.
Draw the treats.

❶

Yogurt
blueberry
cherry
vanilla

Holder
cup   cone

How many different
sandwiches can you make?
Use 1 bread and 1 filling.
Draw the sandwiches.

❷

Bread
pita
wheat

Filling
cheese
vegetable
tuna

© Houghton Mifflin Company. All rights reserved/1

Module 9: Section C, Lesson 14   169

Name _____

144 SKILL PLUS WORKSHEET

Materials: Bag, **7** cubes of one color,
3 cubes of another color

Put the cubes in the bag.
Take **1** cube without looking.
Draw the cube in the table.
Return the cube.
Try it **9** more times.

How many ▨ did you take? _____

How many ☐ did you take? _____

Why do you think you got those numbers?

_____
_____
_____
_____
_____

170   Module 9: Section C, Lesson 15   © Houghton Mifflin Company. All rights reserved/1